IDEAS for CONNECTING CHRIST to HOLIDAYS

Tina Houser

THANKS TO...

- My adoring husband, Ray, for reminding me every day that he loves me, and for encouraging me to continue sharing the craziness that God passes through my brain.
- Bowen and Kendall, the most precious little people in my life. They restore my energy and teach me every time I'm with them. Being "Silly Grandma" to these 6-year-old twins is the best!
- Kevin DeHoff who captures my ideas with his camera and has an enormous amount of patience.
- The Warner Press team, especially Robin and Christian, who have taken the rough work I send them and made a beautiful book from it. You all rock!

Warner Press, Inc
Warner Press and "WP" logo are trademarks of Warner Press, Inc

Holiday Extravaganza: Ideas for Connecting Christ to Holidays
Written by Tina Houser

Warner Press Kids™, an imprint of Warner Press, publishes ministry resources designed to help children grow more deeply in their faith.

Requests for information should be sent to:
Warner Press Inc
1201 East Fifth Street
P.O. Box 2499
Anderson, IN 46012
www.warnerpress.org

Editors: Robin Fogle and Karen Rhodes
Cover & Interior Designer: Christian Elden

ISBN: 978-1-68434-245-7

Printed in USA

TABLE of CONTENTS

A WORD ABOUT

FROM TINA

When it comes to teaching God's Word to kids, I am all about reclaiming time…taking advantage of every moment and utilizing whatever means it takes to engage kids in the Word, help them relate to it, and show them how they can have a lifelong adventure with Jesus as their Savior and Lord. That's what *Holiday Extravaganza* comes down to. It's yet another way for us to step into an opportunity that usually isn't ours to speak truth into.

I'm not advocating that we stop celebrating the traditional holidays of our culture. What I am advocating is utilizing the theme of that holiday to connect with Scripture in some way. There are strong themes in our holidays. Memorial Day, for example, is all about remembering those who have gone before us to give us the freedom we have today. We visit memorials and gravesites to pause for reflection. In much the same way, we see the Old Testament, especially, full of times when an altar was built, when stones were stacked, to create a memorial for future generations. On the 4th of July we celebrate freedom, but as Christ-followers, our freedom is found in the Son of God. Don't raise the white flag and surrender these holidays to the world when you can use each very basic theme and direct the focus to worshipping God. Remember that every day is a day the Lord has created, and we are to rejoice in each one of them (Psalm 118:24).

If you're thinking that we shouldn't bow to these worldly holidays, all I can say is that Jesus used the things of the world to make His points. Remember Matthew 23:27 where He called the Pharisees whitewashed tombs, filled with people's bones? He used the coins of Caesar, as well as terms associated with trades, such as nets, sheep, a yoke, a mustard seed, and a fig tree to teach people. None of these things originally were intended to ignite spiritual conversations. With a little imagination and dwelling on Scripture, you can transform any holiday into a God-honoring day. After all, Jesus came to take the people of the world and transform them into God-honoring people. Surely, we can do that with our holidays.

For each of the holidays included in *Holiday Extravaganza*, you'll find at least four ideas on how to renovate that holiday into a teachable moment for spiritual development. This book is a wonderful resource for the classroom as an adjunct for teachers. It's great for parents to use at home during the holiday as a time to start spiritual conversations. Homeschoolers and kids' clubs will enjoy celebrating holidays in a fresh way. When kids have their friends over and are looking for something to do, older ones can lead themselves in the step-by-step instructions. And don't forget grandparents. They'll become the "cool" grandparents when they have activities with a purpose ready for their favorite little people.

The ideas within these pages are just to get you started. So many of you are crazy creative, and *Holiday Extravaganza* will act as a launching pad for your own ideas. Don't keep them to yourself! I seriously would love to hear how you're giving a new twist to holidays in order to show kids who God is. Please share what you've added to these ideas I've given.

In His incredible joy,

TINA!

tina@tinahouser.net

This is the day that the Lord has made; let us rejoice and be glad in it.

Psalm 118:24 (ESV)

NEW YEAR'S DAY

BUTTERFLY GARDEN

Scripture:

Therefore, if any one is in Christ, he is a new creation; the old has passed away, behold, the new has come (2 Corinthians 5:17, RSV).

Supplies Needed:

- Live Butterfly Garden Kit

Activity

The best place to purchase live butterfly gardens is from insectlore.com. They are not expensive and can be used over and over by just purchasing new caterpillars.

The kids will actually get to watch the metamorphosis process of caterpillars! The super, hands-on, and sensory rich Live Butterfly Garden Kit arrives in a plastic, see-through jar with 4 or 5 caterpillars and a specialty diet. The caterpillars eventually transform into beautiful Painted Lady butterflies, and kids can watch the entire process happen. Once the caterpillars turn into chrysalises, they can be transferred to their reusable, see-through, pop-up mesh butterfly garden habitat.

Let's Talk

A caterpillar goes through a process called metamorphosis, where it turns into a butterfly. The more I find out about this process, the more impact it has as an object lesson of our salvation through Christ. To watch the process is absolutely fascinating! (Remember to take the caterpillars out as soon as they arrive. If you leave them in the box for a couple of weeks, they'll go ahead and turn into butterflies…and that's a story for another time!)

Once the caterpillar wraps itself in the cocoon, its body totally dissolves. It releases enzymes that actually digest its body. The caterpillar doesn't just grow wings and become the body of the butterfly. No, he starts completely over from this goo!

God doesn't just clean us up. No, He makes us brand new—a new creation that flies away from sin and to Him. Many people think of New Year's Day as a time when they get a new start on life. They may decide to make changes—big and small. The fact is, though, that any day can be New Year's Day. You can make changes in your life any day of the year.

Read 2 Corinthians 5:17. *How does the butterfly remind you of what happens when you turn your life over completely to God? You can choose to be a new creation in Christ any day of the year by admitting how you have disobeyed and dishonored God with your sin. Then claim Jesus' death and resurrection as yours—believe that Jesus is God's Son and that He loved you so much He died on the cross for you. Jesus proved He had power over sin by coming out of the grave, even when Satan was sure Jesus was gone for good.*

The caterpillar wrapped itself in the cocoon. What do we "wrap" ourselves in when we claim 2 Corinthians 5:17 for our lives? The caterpillar seemed to be gone for good, but it came out of the cocoon to live a brand new life as a butterfly. You can live a brand new life too!

DO OVERS

Scripture:

The faithful love of the Lord never ends! His mercies never cease. Great is his faithfulness; his mercies begin afresh each morning (Lamentations 3:22-23, NLT).

Supplies Needed:

- 10 random objects (shoe box, book, large plastic cup, mixing bowl, piece of bubble wrap, stick, shoe, tissue box, DVD case, cardboard toilet paper tube)
- 30-second timer

Activity

The kids will work in pairs. Give each pair a set of 10 objects. They have 30 seconds to see how many of the objects they can stack on top of one another. Once the object is in place, though, they cannot move it to rearrange anything. At the end of 30 seconds, indicate time is up and they have to stop. Take note of how many objects they were able to stack.

The leader will yell out, "Do Over!" Take all the objects down and do the same exercise again, giving the same pair of kids the same objects to try to stack in 30 seconds. The same rules apply—no moving an object once it is in place. At the end of 30 seconds, take note of how many objects were stacked this time.

Once again, the leader will yell out, "Do Over!" Take down all the objects, and do the exercise a third time. How many were stacked the third time?

Let's Talk

What happened each time you got a Do Over? Were you able to stack more objects or fewer objects? Each time you did the exercise, you figured out a little more about what worked and what didn't. You kept getting closer to being able to stack all 10 items.

People look at the beginning of a new year and they think, "Oh good. It's a new year. I can do things differently this year. I can start over." But that's not the way God operates. The Bible says that He gives us "do overs" every morning, not just at the beginning of a new year. Read Lamentations 3:22-23 together. *Every morning, God wants to remind you that He loves you again today. It's like He says, "I know you messed up yesterday, but just come to Me. I know you can do better today, and I'll help you." He doesn't HAVE to give us a Do Over, but His mercies are fresh; they're new for us every morning. So God offers us a Do Over, just because He loves us. God knows I can do better. God knows you can do better.*

What does "mercy" mean? It's when you forgive people even though you have the power to punish them for what they've done. When we promise to follow God and then we mess up, we can ask for His forgiveness and get things straightened out again. God gives mercy and forgives us...but He also wants us to follow Him closely and not mess up again. He wants us to keep our eyes on Him, so those things don't continue to happen.

So...what does that look like? Maybe you promised God you would always tell the truth, but when you got in a sticky situation, you tried to get out of it by telling a lie. Yes, you messed up! Admit that to God. He knows you can do better, and He wants to help you keep your word and walk close to Him. His mercies are new every day. What Do Over do you need to ask God for?

PLENTY OF TIME

Scripture:

My times are in Your hand (Psalm 31:15, NASB).

Supplies Needed:

- waxed paper
- play dough
- 30-second timer

Activity

Give the children access to play dough and a piece of waxed paper for their work area. In a mere 30 seconds, their assignment is to make a piece of fruit…any fruit…from the play dough. Make setting the timer very dramatic. The kids will work frantically, but don't let them have any extra time.

Sound a loud signal at the end of the 30 seconds, and everyone should throw up their hands. Keep your hands up! While their hands are still up in the air, instruct the kids that at the signal, they can bring down their hands and SMASH their fruit creation.

Now, let's start over making our fruit. This time the kids will have ample time to finish their fruit the way they like. Take your time and add extra details to make your fruit just the way you want.

Let's Talk

Besides having big parties for New Year's Eve, the big deal about the New Year is making resolutions. This is when we make a new promise to ourselves that we're going to change something—to do better at something. Some people make a resolution to stop smoking, start exercising, or start going to church. It's like they get all panicky and think every good thing they want to do has to happen that very day and week. Most people fail to keep their New Year's resolutions because they want them to happen all at once, immediately.

But time is in God's hands. Read Psalm 31:15. *God is patient. He wants to take you on an adventure and a journey. You're not going to become all that God wants you to be in one day. It takes a lifetime of chasing after Him…wanting to be more like Him. We grow a little bit every time we depend on Him to show Himself to us. It's kind of like when you had time to make your play dough fruit. You kept adding another little detail that you didn't have time to do the first time when you were rushed to come up with something. God has details to add to your life, and He's got all the time in the world to work with you.*

TRAFFIC CONE PLANS

Scripture:

"For I know the plans I have for you," says the Lord. "They are plans for good and not for disaster, to give you a future and a hope" (Jeremiah 29:11, NLT).

Supplies Needed:

- traffic cones

Activity

Form groups of 3 or 4 kids and give each group a traffic cone. Their challenge is to come up with a bunch of different things they could actually use the traffic cone for.

You could:

- Hold it up to your mouth and act like it's a megaphone.
- Wear it as a hat.
- Use it in a ring toss game.
- Stick the pointed end in the ground and fill it with water to make a birdbath or a dog water bowl.

The kids can get as crazy as they like. After a few minutes of sharing in their group, bring them together to share their ideas with other groups.

Let's Talk

We came up with a lot of wild ideas for what you can do with a traffic cone! Were any of them what the traffic cone is actually intended to do? What are you supposed to do with a traffic cone? Many of our ideas were good ones, but the best use of the traffic cone is to let it do what it was made to do—warn people about which way to go.

Read Jeremiah 29:11. *How does this verse remind you of what we were trying to force the traffic cones to do? We were trying to give them a new plan—one they were not intended to do. God has a plan for each of your lives. It's a special plan just for you that will give you hope and the future God wants for you. You may have a good idea, but if it's not God's idea, it's not the best plan.*

As a new year begins, we like to think about OUR plans. But the best plans, the ones that give us an awesome future and hope, are the plans God has in mind. Instead of thinking about what you want for this next year, focus on finding out what God wants for you.

BOBBING LOVE

Scripture:

Love the Lord your God with all your heart and with all your soul and with all your strength (Deuteronomy 6:5, NIV).

Supplies Needed:

- clear drinking glass or small vase
- club soda
- Valentine's conversation heart candy
- teaspoon

Activity

Fill a clear drinking glass or small vase with club soda. The simpler the glass, the easier it is to observe what is happening. Drop a few of the Valentine conversation heart candies into the club soda. The candies should sink. If they don't, it's because they immediately got bubbles on the outside of the candy, so gently tap the candy with a teaspoon to knock some of the bubbles off. Then they should sink. BUT…wait!

The candies will sit at the bottom of the glass for a little bit, gathering bubbles onto the outside of the candy. Once there are enough bubbles clinging to the candy, it will rise to the top. On its ascent, most of the bubbles will come off, which will keep the candy from staying at the top. They will sink to the bottom once again, where they will gather more bubbles and rise to the top. This cycle will continue as long as the club soda stays fizzy. (Anytime the bubbles don't come off on the ascent, you can tap the candy with the teaspoon and gently knock them off.)

Let's Talk

Read Deuteronomy 6:5 together. *Does this verse say, "Love the Lord your God sometimes"? Or "Love the Lord your God when it's convenient"? Or "Love the Lord your God when you feel like it"? Or "Love the Lord your God with some of your heart, soul, and strength"?*

Let's say the Valentine conversation hearts in the club soda represent our commitment to loving the Lord. Is this an example of our total commitment, or is it an example of our on-again/off-again commitment? Our love commitment to God should not go back and forth, back and forth, like the heart candy went up and down, up and down in the glass.

God is committed to loving us ALL the time—during our times of celebration, the frustrating times, the sick times, and the ordinary times. All of it! He commands the same from us if we're going to be His people. He wants us to love Him with everything we have, all the time.

- When do you find yourself going back and forth in your love commitment to God?
- What is it that draws you away from Him, like the bubbles drew the candy to the top?
- What is it that draws you back to Him, like when the bubbles were knocked off the candy?
- What do you need to knock out of the way to show you are totally committed to loving and chasing after God?

HEART WALLPAPER

Scripture:

And now, Israel, what does the Lord your God ask of you but to fear the Lord your God, to walk in obedience to him, to love him, to serve the Lord your God with all your heart and with all your soul (Deuteronomy 10:12, NIV).

Supplies Needed:

- red and pink Post-It notes
- black fine tip markers

Activity

This is a fun and memorable way to serve someone who is going through a prolonged illness or recovering from a devastating loss. Include the kids in choosing whom they will serve in this unique way.

Rather than go store-to-store looking for red and pink Post-It notes, the best way to find them is to purchase online. You will want 200-300 or more! (Yeah, you read that correctly.)

Talk with the kids about ways that God shows love for us during difficult circumstances.

- *What are some truths we know about God's love?*
- *What would be an encouraging reminder for someone to read?*

Write the kids' ideas on a whiteboard for inspiration as they begin working on the hearts.

- God cares.
- God knows what you're feeling.
- God feels your aches.
- God wants to hold you close.
- God can handle your sadness.
- God will give you strength.
- Listen with your heart. God is singing you a lullaby.
- God loves you more than anyone.
- I care about you too.
- You are a child of God.
- You are not alone.
- You are on God's mind every second.
- God is in control.
- God loves you BIG TIME!

Give each child an ample supply (a chunk) of heart Post-It notes and a fine tip marker. They will write a statement on each of the Post-Its. Try not to pull the notes apart because that dilutes the stickiness. Encourage the kids to use their best penmanship and to take their time. This isn't a race to see who can complete the most hearts.

Now comes the really fun part! Arrange a time when the person you are serving with these notes will be away from the room where they spend the most time. This could be a hospital room, assisted living apartment, bedroom, or living room at their home. Get permission for the kids to go in and completely cover that one space with these heart Post-It reminders of God's love. Help the kids to think through places that would be inappropriate and inconvenient for the person, so they won't stick hearts in those places.

Let's Talk

Can you imagine what the person will think when he/she comes into that space? How many times do you think the person will read through the little reminders? How do you think this could change a person's outlook on what he/she is going through?

Read together Deuteronomy 10:12. Talk about how the scripture relates to this activity, and then use the scripture as the basis for your time of prayer. *"I want to love You and serve You, Lord, with all my heart and with all my soul."*

(Continued from previous page)

***Note:** Let the person know that all he/she has to do is give you a call and someone will be there right away to remove all the hearts and stick them together in a stack as a keepsake. The last thing you want to do is create additional work for the person to do!

KRISPIE VALENTINE TREATS

Scripture:

God shows his love for us in that while we were still sinners, Christ died for us (Romans 5:8, ESV).

Supplies Needed:

- 4 c. mini-marshmallows
- 3 T. margarine
- 6 c. Rice Krispies
- large pot
- red food coloring
- 13" x 18" cookie sheet with a lip
- heart-shaped cookie cutter
- tube of decorating icing
- cooking spray
- waxed paper

Activity

Two or three kids can work on a batch of Krispie Treats at a time. Melt the margarine and mini-marshmallows over medium heat in a large pot (preferably nonstick). Add several drops of red food coloring and blend into the melted marshmallows. Add the Rice Krispies and incorporate them quickly into the mixture.

Spray a 13" x 18" cookie sheet with cooking spray. Lightly spray the kids' hands also. They will press the mixture out onto the cookie sheet, so that it is dense. Let this cool completely.

Next, the kids will use a heart-shaped cookie cutter to cut the marshmallow treats. Cut them as close together as possible—most times you can actually share an edge. You don't want to waste any of this luscious goodness! (Of course, someone will need to eat the scraps!) Set the hearts out onto a piece of waxed paper.

Give each child a tube of decorating icing. You can also use some thinned down canned icing in a baggie with a **tiny** corner clipped off. They will write "JESUS" on each of the hearts. But, before they do, have them practice a time or two directly onto the waxed paper or a paper plate. This will help them judge how big their letters are and how their writing will look on the Krispie heart.

Let's Talk

Although we think of Valentine's Day as a time when we express our love to special people in our lives, the ultimate Valentine ever was the one given by our Savior and Lord Jesus. He didn't write it on a glittery card. He didn't put a stamp on it and drop it in the mail. He didn't buy us a box of chocolates or send us flowers. No! He did something far greater to express His love to us. Read Romans 5:8 together. *How did God show His love for us?*

When we disobey God, we separate ourselves from Him. God despised the thought of us being separated from Him so much that He came to earth as one of us—as a person, a man, Jesus. With every step Jesus took, He was showing us how much He loves us. Then He went even further and offered to take the punishment that we deserve because we've disobeyed God. Very simply, all we have to do is believe in the love that He showed us and give ourselves back to Him in gratitude. All we have to do is believe in His one-of-a-kind, very special, "I-love-you" Valentine message.

This Krispie heart doesn't say "Kiss me" or "Sweetheart" or "Love Bug" or "Sweet Pea" on it. It says, "JESUS". His love—His Valentine—is the best one we can receive.

Encourage the kids to share the heart(s) they made with someone, along with telling that person about how Jesus can be his/her forever Valentine.

MUSICAL HEARTS

Scripture:

But now thus says the Lord, he who created you, O Jacob, he who formed you, O Israel: "Fear not, for I have redeemed you; I have called you by name, you are mine" (Isaiah 43:1, ESV).

Supplies Needed:

- red poster board
- music

This activity is especially good for little ones. Cut out a 3" heart from red poster board for each 6-8 children. If you are using something lighter weight than poster board, you will want to laminate it.

Activity

The kids will sit in circles of 6-8 kids. It is difficult for preschoolers to perceive a circle, so sit around the edge of a round rug, mark a circle on the floor with masking tape, or lay a rope down in a circle. Give the poster board heart to one child. The kids will pass the heart around the circle while music plays. When the leader pauses the music, the child with the heart will say, "Jesus loves ________ (their name)." Continue doing this until all the children have gotten a chance to respond at least once.

Say: *I know Jesus would like to hear His name also.* Now, go another round but have the kids say, "Jesus is my Valentine!" If they are still engaging in the activity, you can do a final round with the kids shouting, "Happy Valentine's Day, Jesus!"

Let's Talk

God loves all people—every single person He ever made. He knows you by name. God doesn't just say, "I love all the people I made." He says, "I love Donisha." "I love Denver." "I love Skyla." "I love Muhammad." Read Isaiah 43:1. *Who created you? What does God know about you? He not only knows your name, but He claims you as His.*

Which makes you feel better? When your teacher says, "You have been such a helpful class today" or "______ (child's name), you have been so helpful today." We like to know that someone knows us by name, don't we? Jesus knows you, and better yet, He loves you more than anyone else does. He loves you in monstrous big ways!

On Valentine's Day, we like to tell people, one at a time, by name, that we love them. We don't just say, "Happy Valentine's Day everyone." No, we send a Valentine to each person and tell each person that we love him or her. Jesus wants each one of you to know that He loves you.

According to the Greeting Card Association, approximately 1 billion cards (not including the ones exchanged in school classrooms) are sent yearly, which makes Valentine's Day the second most popular holiday for sending cards.

("History of Valentine's Day")

VALENTINE SCAVENGER HUNT

Supplies Needed:

- red envelopes
- red construction paper hearts

Activity

In this activity you will put clues around the church. When the kids find the first clue, they will look up the verse about love that is written on the outside of the red envelope. They will read the verse out loud and tell briefly in their own words what the verse means to them. Only after that can they open the envelope to find a red heart containing the clue that will take them to the next place.

Try out these clues at the church.

CLUE #1:
Sorry to say, you won't get help from some elves,
But go to the cabinet, and count down 3 shelves.

CLUE #2:
Sometimes it's full, deep, and wide,
But you won't get wet—the clue's on the side.

CLUE #3:
Under the table and on your back,
You'll find the next clue to add to your stack.

CLUE #4:
You've looked high and low and all over the room.
Now go to the closet where we keep the broom.

CLUE #5:
Choose someone to give a high-5;
Then look for the plant that isn't alive.

CLUE #6:
Roses are red and violets are blue.
Go to the check-in to find the next clue.

CLUE #7:
You'll be successful if you just look.
On the desk in the library, find a blue book.

CLUE #8:
You've found all the clues, and we've had loads of fun. Get a drink at the fountain, and then you are done.

These are scriptures that can be written on the outside of the envelopes.

- 1 John 4:8
- John 3:16
- 1 Corinthians 13:4-7
- 1 Corinthians 13:13
- Ephesians 4:2
- 1 Peter 4:8
- 1 John 4:7
- John 15:13
- Colossians 3:14
- Proverbs 10:12
- 1 John 3:16-18
- Romans 12:9
- Mark 12:31
- Romans 13:10

There are a couple of other options where you could use this same idea.

Option 2:

This activity could easily be turned into a family Valentine event that actually could take families all around the community. They would go armed with their Bibles, read the clue, find the destination, discuss the verse, open their envelope for the next destination, and then move on to discover the next location.

Option 3:

Instead of doing the search around the church, make the clues for places around your home (inside the dishwasher, in Mom's make-up bag, down in one of Dad's shoes, in a toy chest).

Origin of Valentine's Day

The truth is, we can't say with certainty what the origin of Valentine's Day is, but we do know that it had something to do with St. Valentine.

One legend has it that Emperor Claudius II found that single men made better soldiers; therefore, he outlawed marriage. Valentine refused to stop performing marriages and continued to do so in secret, because he believed in the love that God placed between a man and woman. When found out, Claudius ordered Valentine put to death.

The other prominent legend is that Valentine helped Christians escape Roman persecution. When imprisoned himself for helping the Christians, he fell in love with the jailer's daughter. On the day of his execution, he wrote her a love note and signed it "from your Valentine." This type of note later became known as a Valentine ("History of Valentine's Day").

Both legends are rooted in a belief in the One True God, who loved beyond our imaginations and sent His Son. Neither legend would have been passed down if Valentine had not been committed to God's love.

APPLE SHAMROCKS

Scripture:

And when Jesus was baptized, immediately he went up from the water, and behold, the heavens were opened to him, and he saw the Spirit of God descending like a dove and coming to rest on him; and behold, a voice from heaven said, "This is my beloved Son, with whom I am well pleased" (Matthew 3:16-17, ESV).

Supplies Needed:

- plastic disposable plates
- green craft paint
- water
- red delicious apples
- sharp knife
- white poster paper
- forks
- small paint brush

Activity

Add a little water to some green craft paint to thin it somewhat. Spread the paint in a thin layer onto a plastic disposable plate.

Remove the stem from a red delicious apple. Use a large sharp knife to cut the apple in two, from top to bottom. (We suggest the delicious apple because, when cut in two, it has a noticeable indention in the top and bottom.)

The kids will press the cut-side of the apple into the paint and then press it 3 times onto a piece of white poster paper to make the 3 leaves of a shamrock. The small end of the apple should be toward the center of the cluster, with the larger end of the apple as the ends of the leaves.

It's a little difficult to hold onto the apple because it's curved, so before dipping it in the paint, stick a fork into the skin-side of the half-apple. Now you have a handle.

Use a paintbrush to make a swish for the stem of the shamrock.

Let's Talk

We sometimes get confused about the difference between a shamrock and a 4-leaf clover. The 4-leaf clover is just a rare thing that happens with clover, and finding one is supposed to bring you good luck. There is no special power in a 4-leaf clover, and it actually has nothing to do with St Patrick's Day. But the shamrock does.

St. Patrick used the shamrock, which has 3 leaves, as an object lesson when he was trying to explain to people that God is Three in One. That's a difficult thing to understand! God is God the Father, God the Son, and God the Holy Spirit. All three are God. Sometimes we talk about God as Father and Creator of everything. Sometimes we talk about God as coming to earth in the form of a man, Jesus. Sometimes we talk about God as living inside us, helping us to live the way God wants us to, and that's God the Holy Spirit.

Read Matthew 3:16-17. Find the mention of God the Father, God the Son (Jesus), and God the Holy Spirit.

When you think of your mom, she is one person, but she is different things to different people at different times. She may be an employee if she has a job. She is someone's daughter. She is a friend to someone. She is your mom. You don't think of her as an employee; you think of her as your mom. Her friend doesn't think of her as her daughter. She is all of these things, but she's still one person. That's kind of how it is with God. He is God the Father, God the Son, and God the Holy Spirit.

- *When you think about God the Father, what goes through your mind? What is God like as the Creator and Father of everything and everyone?* Point to one of the leaves of the shamrock.
- *What do you think of when you hear the name of Jesus?* Point to another leaf of the shamrock.
- *What does the Holy Spirit mean to you? How does the Holy Spirit make your life different?* Point to the third leaf on the shamrock.

Encourage the kids to use their apple-painted shamrock to tell someone else about God being Three in One. That's a challenge!

Let's Talk

Even though St. Patrick had been taken by pirates as a slave to Ireland as a teenager, he was able to escape and make his way back to Britain. During his years as a slave, he came to know Jesus as his personal Savior. Years later, he had dreams where he saw the Irish people calling him to come back and teach them about Jesus. God used these dreams to let Patrick know that he was being sent back to Ireland to preach the Good News of Jesus. Once back in Ireland, he walked all over the country—along the shores and through the towns, in churches and on the streets—telling anyone who would listen about Jesus.

Read Romans 10:15 together. *How does this verse remind you of what we know about St. Patrick? He preached because God sent him to do that. The people who accepted the message of Jesus must have been very glad that Patrick walked all over their country. In their eyes, I bet his feet were beautiful!*

GOOD NEWS FEET

Scripture:

And how can anyone preach unless they are sent? As it is written: "How beautiful are the feet of those who bring good news!" (Romans 10:15, NIV).

Supplies Needed:

- 4-ounce paper cups
- rubber bands
- paper clips
- paper
- pencils
- construction paper arrows

Game

Prepare for the game by making a carrying cup for each child. This cup will attach to one of his/her feet. Poke a hole in the bottom of a small cup. Thread a loop of a rubber band through the hole, from the outside to the inside. Attach a paper clip to the rubber band loop that is on the inside of the cup. Now, when you tug on the rubber band from the outside, the paper clip will keep the rubber band from pulling out through the hole. The rubber band on the outside of the cup should be big enough to pull over the toe of a child's shoe. (Depending on the age of your children, you will have to adjust the size of rubber band you use.)

What piece of good news about Jesus do you think Patrick told the people? The kids will write their good news on a small piece of paper. Give each child one of the carrying cups that you prepared beforehand to attach to one of his/her feet. Fold the Good News paper into a small square so that it will fit down in the cup. Lay a trail of arrows on the floor all around the room. How many you use will depend on the age of your kids—the older the kids, the more arrows you can use.

The kids will follow the arrows to carry their Good News paper in their cup. Once they reach the destination, they will shake out their paper and say, "I bring good news of Jesus!" You can set up several trails for kids to do at the same time, or you can start the next player once the first one gets about halfway through the course.

SHAMROCK CUPCAKES

Scripture:

But you will receive power when the Holy Spirit comes on you; and you will be my witnesses in Jerusalem, and in all Judea and Samaria, and to the ends of the earth (Acts 1:8, NIV).

Supplies Needed:

- white cake mix and ingredients
- can of white frosting
- green food coloring
- paper cupcake liners
- cupcake baking tins
- baking tools
- craft sticks
- aluminum foil
- gallon food storage bag
- scissors
- Styrofoam bowls (or some other container for safe transport)

Activity

The kids will make some shamrock cupcakes. Make sure you have enough for each child to make at least 2 cupcakes. Mix up some boxed white cake mix and add lots of green food coloring. (Add 5 drops at a time until it reaches the shade you desire.) Put the batter into a gallon food storage bag.

The kids will prepare the cupcake baking tins by putting in paper liners. Roll up 3 small balls of aluminum foil. Push these down between the paper and the tin in 3 places, evenly spaced. This should give the cupcake liner a shape that resembles the 3 leaves of a shamrock.

Clip the corner on the batter bag and pipe the batter into the cups. This works much better… with much less mess…than trying to spoon in the batter. Bake the cupcakes and let them cool.

Mix some green food coloring into a can of white icing. Using a craft stick, the kids will ice their cupcakes (at least 2 of them), swirling the icing in a circle on each of the leaves to make them look more like individual leaves.

Let's Talk

The shamrock reminds us of the Trinity. Trinity means that God, although He is one God, is three—God the Father, God the Son, and God the Spirit. The legend is that St. Patrick used the shamrock to help tell others about God. Many people don't know that St. Patrick's Day is to honor a man who wanted more than anything to honor God with his life. He wanted to tell others, especially in Ireland, how much God loved them.

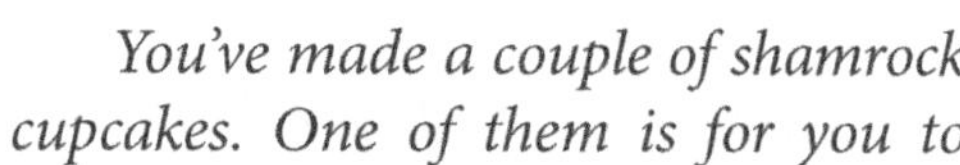

You've made a couple of shamrock cupcakes. One of them is for you to

enjoy. The others are for you to give away. But we don't want to just hand the cupcake to someone and walk off. Your challenge is to give the cupcake to someone other than a family member and tell him or her something you learned about St. Patrick. (He was a missionary. He loved God. He went to Ireland to tell people about God.)

YOU MEANT IT FOR HARM

Scripture:

You intended to harm me, but God intended it all for good. He brought me to this position so I could save the lives of many people (Genesis 50:20, NLT).

Supplies Needed:

- coins
- crown
- scoop
- corn meal
- bowl
- jar
- crackers

Story Time

Tell the kids this shortened version of the story of Joseph:

Joseph's brothers were jealous of him because Joseph was his father's favorite son. One day, the brothers had the opportunity to sell Joseph to some merchants who were going to Egypt…and they did. They sold their brother as a slave!

While in prison in Egypt, God helped Joseph. Joseph was able to tell people what their dreams meant. The king had an unusual dream and called Joseph to help him understand it. The dream was about 7 years of good crops that would be followed by 7 years of no harvest. The king needed someone to oversee storing up the food for the time when there would be no crops. The king was very pleased with Joseph for helping him. He chose Joseph to oversee the food storage and made him second in command of the kingdom. Only the king had more power than Joseph.

When the horrible time of famine (no food) came, Joseph's brothers ran out of food in the far off country. They heard there was food in Egypt, so they went there to see if they could get some. That's when they discovered their brother, whom they had sold years ago. They were frightened that Joseph would still be very angry with them, but Joseph told them that what they had intended to harm him actually ended up being a good thing. He was now able to help them!

Let's Talk

If you have not already done so, share the story of St. Patrick. He had been taken as a slave into a strange country. But while in that strange land of Ireland, he came to know the Lord. He was able to escape, but years later he went back to Ireland to teach the people about Jesus. Many people began to follow the Lord because of him.

Read Genesis 50:20. *How does the story of Joseph remind you of the story of St. Patrick? Both were taken away to a different country to be slaves. Both of them took a bad experience and made something good out of it. Joseph was able to rescue his brothers from hunger, and St. Patrick was able to tell the Irish about God.*

Think of a bad experience you've had or maybe are having right now. How can you use that bad experience for good? If you give it to God and trust Him, He will show you how good can come out of it. You can believe Genesis 50:20 is true for your life.

Game

Set up 4 stations. The kids will run to each station in order, perform the action described, and SAY the phrase. They will leave the prop at that station before heading to the next one. This will help them remember the story of Joseph.

STATION #1:
Count out 10 coins and stack them. Say: "Joseph was sold into slavery by his brothers."

STATION #2:
Put on a crown. Say: "Joseph helped the king understand a dream."

STATION #3:
Put 2 scoops of corn meal from a bowl into a sack. Say: "The king put Joseph in charge of storing up food."

STATION #4:
Eat a cracker and rub your stomach. Say: "Joseph helped his brothers when they needed food."

Origin of St. Patrick's Day

Although some of the details vary between historians, most of them agree on this information about St. Patrick's Day:

The man we have come to know as St. Patrick, the patron saint of Ireland, was actually from Britain. In the late 4th century, when he was just a teenager, he was captured and taken to Ireland as a slave. Although it was awful that he was a slave, he became a Christian during this time. After 6 years, he was able to escape and made his way back to Britain.

Something strange happened a few years later. After returning to Great Britain, Patrick started having dreams, and in those dreams the Irish were calling him to return to them and teach them about Christ. For years these dreams recurred, and finally when he was in his 60s, Patrick went back to the country where he had been a slave in order to tell the people about Jesus. For decades he wandered around Ireland, preaching and building churches. Ireland was forever changed because of his missionary work there.

Most historians agree that, even though the Catholic Church canonized him, it is doubtful that Patrick was Catholic. His writings and records of what he said place him much closer to the Protestant Church.

He believed the Father, Son, and Holy Spirit are one. A legend says he held a shamrock, which has 3 leaves, in his hand as an object lesson of sorts, to represent that the Three are One—Father, Son, and Holy Spirit. The shamrock became the national symbol of Ireland, and St. Patrick's Day is celebrated on March 17.

GOTCHA

Scriptures:

He isn't here! He is risen from the dead, just as he said would happen. Come, see where his body was lying (Matthew 28:6, NLT).

O death, where is your victory? O death, where is your sting? (1 Corinthians 15:55, NLT).

Supplies Needed:

- bowls
- cereal
- milk
- spoons
- freezer

Activity

Beforehand, fill several bowls about halfway with cereal and pour milk over the top. Freeze these completely. Then, right before you start the lesson, add a little more fresh cereal and a splash of milk to each bowl to disguise what is underneath.

Place the bowls, along with spoons, on a table at the front of the room. Choose a child for each bowl, and pretend you are going to have a contest to see who can eat their bowl of cereal the fastest. When you give the signal for them to begin, the kids will competitively force their spoons into their bowls, only to discover the frozen cereal. That's when you can yell, "Gotcha! April Fools!"

Let's Talk

It's pretty funny to pull a harmless prank on someone. What makes for a good April Fool's Day prank? You have to do something that the person is totally not expecting. You have to surprise them with what happens. Did our contestants expect to stick their spoons down into frozen cereal? No, that was ridiculous. Nobody freezes a bowl of cereal! Completely unexpected!

God did something completely unexpected also. In fact, it wasn't just that people didn't expect it—Satan didn't expect it. It was the ultimate April Fool's surprise on Satan himself. When Jesus died on the cross and then was put in the grave, what did Satan expect? He expected Jesus to stay there! Read Matthew 28:6. *This is what the angel said to the women when they came to the grave. They expected to go to the grave and put spices on Jesus' dead body, but surprise of all surprises, He wasn't there!*

When Jesus gave up His last breath, what do you think Satan was thinking? I bet he was doing his happy dance and bragging about his victory. Now read 1 Corinthians 15:55. *While Satan is dancing around, God interrupts and says, "Oh really? What kind of victory are you celebrating? My Son is no longer dead." Even the mighty power of death couldn't keep Jesus down. This was the ultimate "Gotcha!"*

What do you think you would've said to Satan if you were the first one to let him know that Jesus was alive?

Anytime you are faced with Satan's tricks, you can throw them right back at him and say, "God is my power, and He raised Jesus from the dead. Gotcha, Satan!"

POTATO PULL

Scripture:

Then he told them a story: "A rich man had a fertile farm that produced fine crops. He said to himself, 'What should I do? I don't have room for all my crops.' Then he said, 'I know! I'll tear down my barns and build bigger ones. Then I'll have room enough to store all my wheat and other goods. And I'll sit back and say to myself, "My friend, you have enough stored away for years to come. Now take it easy! Eat, drink, and be merry!"'

But God said to him, 'You fool! You will die this very night. Then who will get everything you worked for?'"

Yes, a person is a fool to store up earthly wealth but not have a rich relationship with God.
(Luke 12:16-21, NLT).

Supplies Needed:

- potatoes
- Bibles

Activity

For each pair of kids, you will need an object they can wrap their hands around securely. This may sound weird, but an object that works very well is a potato, and they don't bruise easily. (You also may use empty pop cans.) The kids will work with a partner on this activity. One partner will clinch his/her hand around a potato as tightly as possible. The other partner will try to pry his/her fingers away from the potato. Take turns so that both kids get a chance to be the one who is holding tight and the one who is prying away the fingers.

Let's Talk

If your potato had been a burning piece of charcoal, would you have held on so tightly? Did you know that the Bible tells us to grab hold of some things and to hold others loosely? Some things we should store up, and others we shouldn't.

Read Luke 12:16-21, the parable of the man who stored up in barns, as the kids follow along in their Bibles.

- *Why was the man foolish?*
- *What makes a man wise?*
- *Is there anything that you "store up," that you make more important than knowing God?*
- *Are you holding on tightly to something?*

Things are not important in God's eyes. He loves the poor man just as much as He loves the rich man. When God welcomes us into heaven, He's not going to have someone help us move our stuff into the place He is preparing for us. Our stuff stays here. It's our relationship with God that matters.

SPEWING FOOLISHNESS

Scripture:

Do to others as you would like them to do to you (Luke 6:31, NLT).

Supplies Needed:

- 2 1-liter bottles
- water
- 2 balloons
- pushpin
- duct tape

Activity

Say: *Did you know that I can put a water balloon inside this 1-liter bottle? Here, let me show you how.*

Blow up a balloon to stretch it out a bit and then let the air out. Push the balloon down into the bottle and secure the lip of the balloon around the top of the bottle. It will be hanging down inside the bottle now. Try blowing into it. Nothing will happen.

Use a pushpin to poke a hole in the bottom of the bottle. Now blow into the balloon and it will inflate. Cover the hole with some duct tape before removing your mouth from the balloon. The balloon will stay inflated. Now, add some water to the balloon. Carefully, pull the lip of the balloon away from the mouth of the bottle and tie it off. The main part of the balloon is down inside the bottle. Once it's tied, you can drop it down inside the bottle. Yep, there you go, a water balloon inside a bottle!

Now let's go one more step. With another 1-liter bottle and another balloon, do the same thing as before to fill the water balloon, BUT this time just let it hang there. Do not tie it off.

Bring someone over close to the bottle, and tell him to look down in the balloon to make sure there is water in it. Then say, "You don't want to do that. You should probably step back." As soon as they step back, pull the duct tape off the bottom of the bottle, and the water in the balloon will spew out in a fountain.

Let's Talk

I could've pulled the duct tape off when you were looking down in the balloon. What would've happened to you if I had done that? You would've gotten your face soaking wet! Everybody would've laughed at you. But I stopped before I did that. I knew I wouldn't want to get wet in front of everyone, and I sure wouldn't want them laughing at me, so I didn't do it to you.

No one likes to look like a fool. On April Fool's Day we play silly tricks on people, mostly just to see how creative we can be and what we can actually make happen. But sometimes it embarrasses people in front of someone they know or in front of complete strangers. How does that feel? Read Luke 6:31 together. *What does Jesus say about what we do to other people? We should treat others the same way we want them to treat us. I wouldn't want to be embarrassed in front of the entire group, so I didn't want to embarrass you in front of the group.*

In what other ways can you live out Luke 6:31?

WHAT A MESS!

Scripture:

Anyone who listens to my teaching and follows it is wise, like a person who builds a house on solid rock. Though the rain comes in torrents and the floodwaters rise and the winds beat against that house, it won't collapse because it is built on bedrock. But anyone who hears my teaching and doesn't obey it is foolish, like a person who builds a house on sand. When the rains and floods come and the winds beat against that house, it will collapse with a mighty crash
(Matthew 7:24-27, NLT).

Supplies Needed:

- window cleaner
- chocolate pudding
- canned dog food
- spoons
- liquid laundry detergent
- jelly
- tarp or wading pool
- an adult the kids love

Activity

Beforehand, arrange for a volunteer (an adult the kids love to hang out with) to be doused in all kinds of messy stuff. This volunteer should bring a couple of towels and a change of clothes. He/she will sit or stand on a tarp or in a kiddie pool. Because all the kids will want to be chosen for this, put their names on pieces of paper and draw out a name each time you need a participant (or use some other random way of selecting them).

The leader will read a foolish way to use one of the ingredients from the list below. Choose a participant who will have the opportunity to commit the foolish act on the willing volunteer you have prearranged. (Feel free to change some of these ingredients, according to what you have available.) After performing the foolish thing, ask the child who did it what wise thing they could've done with that same ingredient.

CHOCOLATE PUDDING is meant to go in your mouth. It would be foolish to put it on your arms. (The child will smear chocolate pudding on the adult volunteer's arms.)

WINDOW CLEANER is meant to go on your windows. It would be foolish to squirt it on your feet. (The child will squirt the window cleaner on the adult volunteer's feet.)

DOG FOOD is meant to go in the dog dish. It would be foolish to use it to wash your hands. (The child will dish out the dog food in the volunteer's hands.)

LAUNDRY DETERGENT is meant to go in the washing machine. It would be foolish to fill your pockets with it. (The child will pour detergent in the volunteer's pockets.)

JELLY is meant to go on a sandwich. It would be foolish to put it between your toes. (The child will smoosh jelly between the volunteer's toes.)

TOMATO JUICE is meant for a refreshing drink. It would be foolish to wash your hair with it. (The child will pour tomato juice on the volunteer's head.)

Let's Talk

These things may have sounded so foolish that they were ridiculous. Who in the world would do these things?

Go over the parable of the wise man and the foolish man by reading it straight from Matthew 7:24-27. *How does Jesus describe a wise person? Someone who listens to what Jesus teaches but also follows it. How does Jesus describe a foolish person? Someone who hears what He teaches but doesn't obey it. Did the storm treat the two men differently? No, both got rained on. Everybody, no matter if we are Christ-followers or not, will go through trouble—what we sometimes call "storms of life." The person who follows what Jesus says will come through it with God's help—the Solid Rock—and will live with Him for eternity.*

Living according to God's Word is not a difficult thing to understand, but some of the ways that people choose to live away from God's Word are just as ridiculous and foolish as the things we just did.

Give your volunteer a big round of applause!

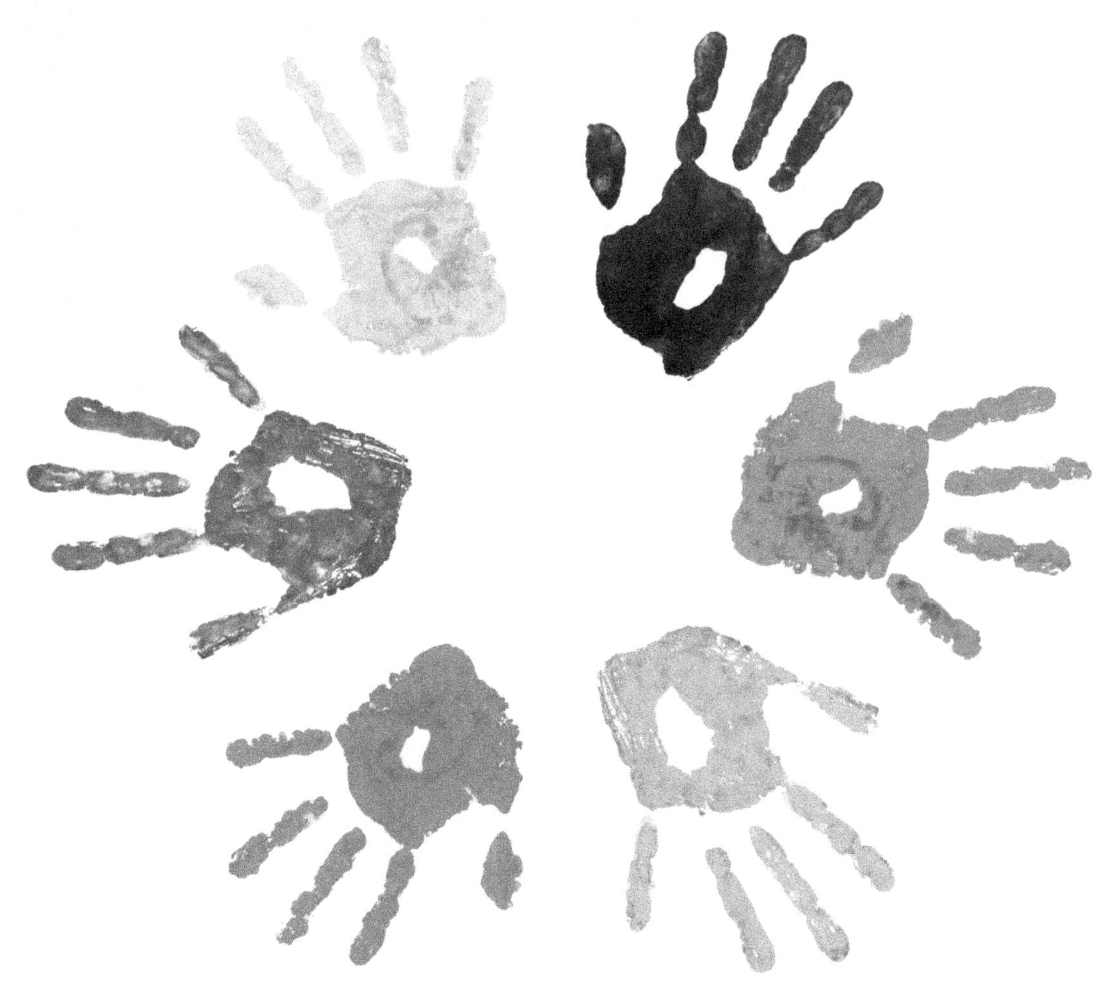

AFTER DARK EGG HUNT

Scriptures:

Then Jesus again spoke to them, saying, "I am the Light of the world; he who follows Me will not walk in the darkness, but will have the Light of life" (John 8:12, NASB).

You are the light of the world.... Let your light shine before men in such a way that they may see your good works, and glorify your Father who is in heaven (Matthew 5:14 &16, NASB).

Supplies Needed:

- plastic eggs (good quality ones)
- glow-in-the-dark bracelets
- buckets/containers

Activity

You'll need to prepare this egg hunt when it is almost dark outside. (The day before, test one of the glow-in-the-dark bracelets to see how long it will continue to glow. That should give you an idea of how much time you'll need for assembling your eggs and having the hunt.) Open all the eggs. Crack a glow-in-the-dark bracelet and wind it to fit inside an egg. Snap the egg shut. If it's a good quality egg, it will stay shut. If not, you'll need to add a small piece of clear packing tape. (Works much better than regular tape.) Now you have glow-in-the-dark eggs. Cool!

Take the kids out of sight while helpers hide all the eggs. An area with bushes and tall grass is really great for this activity. Give the kids some kind of gathering bucket or container. Set them loose to discover the glow-in-the-dark eggs. Once all the eggs have been retrieved, hand the eggs over to the "hiders" and move the kids out of sight again.

While the eggs are being re-hidden, talk with the kids. Read John 8:12 slowly together. Then ask these questions:

- *How is Jesus like these glow-in-the-dark eggs?*
- *It's dark out here! We all walk in a spiritual darkness—a darkness that's inside us. This kind of darkness comes when we are separated from God by our disobedience—our sin. How does it feel to be in complete darkness?*
- *Jesus said He is the Light of the world, so how do we get out of darkness and see Jesus, the Light?*
- *When we walk with Jesus every day of our lives, what do we have inside us?*

When the eggs are hidden, send the kids out for a second time to gather the glow-in-the-dark eggs. Once they are gathered, do like before, and take the kids to a separate area while the "hiders" place the eggs for a third time. Read Matthew 5:14 and 16.

- *What do these verses say about light? They say WE are the light in this world. When we are light, we glorify God.*
- *How are we like the glow-in-the-dark eggs?*

- *How can you be light in this world? Be specific. (Stop and listen to someone who is upset. Pray with someone right in the middle of a situation. Give God credit throughout the day, wherever you are and with whomever. Refuse to be part of things that God would not be proud of. Tame your anger, frustration, and smart remarks.)*

When the eggs are hidden again, send the kids out for another hunt. Continue with rounds of hiding and hunting as long as the kids are engaged and/ or the eggs continue to glow in the dark.

HAMMERING THE SPIKE

Scripture:

Finally Pilate handed him over to them to be crucified. So the soldiers took charge of Jesus. Carrying his own cross, he went out to the place of the Skull (which in Aramaic is called Golgotha). There they crucified him, and with him two others—one on each side and Jesus in the middle (John 19:16-18, NIV).

Supplies Needed:

- largest spike you can find
- 4" x 4" plank
- large hammer

Activity

When this activity is set up in a large room, it has even more impact because there will be a bit of an echo. Before the kids arrive, drive a large spike into the 4" x 4" plank to get it started. Spikes can be found at a home improvement store for less than a dollar each.

The kids will individually read aloud John 19:16-18, but just to themselves. If you have nonreaders, either record the passage so they can listen to it or post someone at the activity to read the passage to them. Let the child follow along with his/her finger on the words as it's being read.

Once the children have the scripture in mind, each child will get the opportunity to hammer the spike into the wood one time. It is a big spike, and they need to hit it hard. Hitting the spike is only part of the experience. The sound that it makes is what cuts to the core. It can be quite an emotional sound.

Let's Talk

Although you and I were not there that day when Jesus was nailed to the cross, He was actually thinking of us. Describe what you think Jesus felt each time the spike was hit again. *No one begged Jesus to die on the cross for us. No, He offered to do it because He loves us so much! We have all disobeyed God and let the devil talk us into things. Every single one of us has. When we sin and disobey God, we are separated from Him because He is holy and cannot tolerate sin. God is just and must punish sin.*

It totally amazes me that God, knowing we must be punished for turning our backs on Him, offered to accept Jesus' cruel death as payment. Our sin separates us from God, and no number of good deeds is going to get us back to Him. BUT when we believe in what Jesus did on the cross and that He had the power to come back from death, then God welcomes us back. He says, "If you truly believe I love you enough to send Jesus to have those spikes driven into His hands and that I would not let Him stay dead, then welcome back to Me."

Hearing the spike hit by the hammer may be a terrible sound. But it is a sound, that if we believe in what it means, will bring us back to the One who created us and loves us as His own sons and daughters.

IT ALL HAPPENED AT DINNER

Scriptures:

Luke 22:7-38 and John 13:1-30

Supplies Needed:

- 3-step stool/ladder
- bucket of water
- towel
- rubber feet markers
- bowl
- crackers

Activity

A sequencing relay is when you set up 3 or 4 stations, each with a simple prop that pertains to the story. Leave as much space as possible between these stations, and create as many duplicates of the entire relay as your space will allow. The more duplicates you have, the more teams you can create, and the more kids can be engaged at the same time. Also, at each station, the kids will need to do something with the prop and say a simple statement they HAVE to make that connects to the story. They cannot move on in the relay until they have used the prop and made the statement.

For little ones, this is a great opportunity to recruit some teenagers as helpers to give small prompts as to what they should do and say at each station. The others waiting to go will be listening intently, so they can get it on their own when their turn comes.

Each team is assigned a relay set-up. At a signal, one kid from each team will run to the first station, use the prop, and make the statement. Once that's done, they set the prop back where they found it and run as fast as they can to the second station. There they will use the prop and make the statement, replacing the prop when they're done. They continue doing this as fast as they can until they've completed all the stations. This will have led them through the main points of the story. They run back to their team and tag the next player, who begins his/her run through the stations.

Sequencing Relay for the Last Supper

STATION #1:

- Prop is a 3-step stool/ladder.
- The child will climb the ladder and at the top say, "They went upstairs for supper."

STATION #2:

- Props are a bucket of water, a towel, and some rubber feet. (If you don't have these, you really should add them to your resources. They can be used in a huge number of ways. Hands and feet markers can be purchased at usgames.com, $9.99/dozen.)
- The child picks up one of the rubber feet and dips it in the bucket of water. As the child is drying it off, he/she will say, "Jesus washed their feet."

Station #3:

- Prop is a bowl of broken crackers.
- The child will take one piece of cracker and eat it. When the child has completely swallowed, he/she will say, "Jesus said, 'This is my body. Remember Me.'"

Station #4:

- Prop is an open door. It really works great if you have a room that has 2 doors in it. That way the child can run out one door and back in the other one.
- As the child runs out of the room, he/she will say, "Judas left!"

It is absolutely amazing how this relay will cement the story in children's minds. Do not let them move on to another station, though, without saying the statement. That is key to connecting the action with what occurred in Scripture.

THORNS AND JEWELS

Scriptures:

The soldiers twisted together a crown of thorns and put it on his head. They clothed him in a purple robe and went up to him again and again, saying, "Hail, king of the Jews!" And they slapped him in the face (John 19:2-3, NIV).

And when the Great Shepherd appears, you will receive a crown of never-ending glory and honor (1 Peter 5:4, NLT).

Supplies Needed:

- real crown of thorns
- small grapevine wreath
- wooden toothpicks
- colored rhinestones
- glue

Activity

You will need a real crown of thorns. These can be ordered online fairly inexpensively (under $15). They are made from the only thorn bush that grows in or around Jerusalem, so it's very likely this is what Jesus' crown looked like.

Show a real crown of thorns. *When Jesus was dying on the cross, they made fun of Him by calling Him the King of the Jews. Kings wear crowns, so they made a crown out of a thorny vine and pushed it down onto Jesus' head.* Read together John 19:2-3. Give the kids time to react to this real crown of thorns and what it must've felt like to have that pushed into His forehead. They may want to touch some of the thorns to realize how very pointy they are…just caution them to do that gently.

Jesus suffered through all of this for the people of that day, for us, for all the people who lived in between, and for the people who will be born into this world. When we look at the cross and at this crown, you can be reminded and I can be reminded that each thorn can represent how we have disobeyed God and walked away from Him.

Place the grapevine wreath flat on a table. (This is NOT the crown of thorns, but a plain grapevine wreath.) The participants will think of some way they have disobeyed God—how they have sinned. Then they will wedge a toothpick down into the weave of the grapevine. Once they have all done this, then move into the second part.

Jesus took all this punishment—the cross and the thorny crown—so that we could be with God forever. When we claim and accept Jesus' sacrifice, we get the promise of being with God forever in heaven.

Turn the grapevine over. *What do you think heaven will be like?* The kids can finish one of these two sentences:

- Heaven will have no more _____________. (sickness, bullies, curse words, divorce, hatred, wars)
- Heaven will be _____________. (beautiful, happy, full of dancing and singing, more than we can imagine)

As they finish their sentence and make their statement, the kids will glue a colored rhinestone jewel onto this side of the crown. *Isn't this jeweled crown beautiful? The Bible tells us that Jesus has gone to get a place ready for us, and that we will have a heavenly crown. I have no idea what it will look like!* Read 1 Peter 5:4 together.

As you wrap up, flip the crown from the side showing thorns to the other side showing jewels. *Jesus wore this crown, and each thorn represents how we have hurt God. The other side is the crown we will get to wear because Jesus wore the thorny crown.*

CRYSTAL TREE

Scripture:

Oh, the joys of those who...delight in the law of the Lord, meditating on it day and night. They are like trees planted along the riverbank, bearing fruit each season (Psalm 1:1-3, NLT).

Supplies Needed:

- Mrs. Stewart's Bluing (found in detergent aisle)
- salt
- ammonia
- lightweight cardboard
- water
- measuring spoons
- food coloring
- bowl

Instructions for Experiment

- From the lightweight plain cardboard (not corrugated or printed), cut 2 identical Christmas tree shapes (no trunk) that are about 3" at the base and about 4" tall.
- On one tree, make a slit from the center of the bottom to halfway up the tree. On the other tree, make a slit from the top point of the tree to halfway down the tree. This will enable you to slide the 2 pieces together so that the tree will stand by itself and will have 4 extensions.
- In a bowl mix 1 T. water, 1 T. of Mrs. Stewart's Bluing, 1 T. salt, and 1½ t. ammonia. Add 2 or 3 drops of food coloring for whatever color tree you would like. (Make sure the bowl you are using has a flat bottom big enough for the tree to stand in.)
- Set the tree down in the mixture and then don't move it.
- Now wait! (This is perhaps the most difficult part of the experiment.) In a few hours crystals should start appearing on the cardboard tree. Within 24 hours it will be covered with crystals.
- If you want the tree to grow more crystals, mix up another batch of the water, ammonia, salt, and bluing to add to the bowl.

Let's Talk

Not only are we supposed to care for the world God created, but we are to learn from it also. On this Earth Day, it is interesting to see how the Bible gives us lessons using nature. We find it over and over—object lessons using rivers and mountains and sheep and rocks...and trees, like in the verses we're going to look at today. Read together Psalm 1:1-3.

The Bible gives us a picture of a tree that is planted by the riverbank. It gets water there and sunshine. Because it gets water and sun, it grows and bears fruit. We are like the tree when we meditate on God's Word day and night...when we read it...when we talk about it...when we ask questions about it...when we soak it up!

Here we have a paper tree. Show a plain cardboard tree that hasn't been put in the bluing solution. *We feed the tree with this special food because you know that paper trees need a different kind of food (chuckle). We need a different kind of food too. Our spiritual food is the Bible, the Word of God. Because we give the tree the special good food it needs, the tree grows.* Pull out the tree that has been growing for a day with all the crystals on it. *It is healthy and beautiful and bears fruit! When we stay in the Word, we grow spiritually.*

We can grow by putting good stuff in and feeding our spirits. We fed our little paper tree. Yes? We fed it with the special paper tree food. The person who grows spiritually "delights" in the Lord. "Delights" means that we enjoy it. It makes us happy. It satisfies us. Do you enjoy the Lord? Does He make you happy? Does He satisfy you? To grow like God wants us to, we must think about what His Word says all the time. It's in our minds and our hearts—not just sometimes, but all the time. In every decision, you consider if it goes along with God's Word. If you do these things, you will be like the crystal tree…growing into something magnificent!

EARTHY SCAVENGER HUNT

Scripture

Through him all things were made; without him nothing was made that has been made (John 1:3, NIV).

Supplies Needed:

- collection bag for each group
- 2 or 3 small containers for each bag
- copies of the Scavenger Hunt verses
- pencils
- Bibles

Activity

Kids love scavenger hunts, and this one offers a great way to exercise their Bible skills too! Form groups of 2 or 3 kids. Each group will be given a collection bag that has a few small containers in it. They will also need a copy of the Scavenger Hunt verses, a pencil, and a Bible for each child. Determine the boundaries of the scavenger hunt and make sure the kids are clear on where they can and cannot go.

Make a Scavenger Hunt Sheet, listing the verses below (and any others that you would like to add). Put a blank line next to each verse. Do not include the item that is listed in parentheses—that is for your convenience and information only. If any of these items are not available in the designated area, then take them off the Hunt Sheet. In any order they choose, the kids will look up one verse together and find an item in that verse that is something God created. It is something that He put on this Earth. They should write the object in the space next to the verse and then find that object to put in their collection bag. Once they have that object, then they can look up another verse and do the same thing. The objective of the exercise is to look up all the verses and find something God created to put in their collection bag from each verse.

- Matthew 16:18 (rock)
- 1 Peter 1:24 (grass/flowers)
- Job 14:2 (flower)
- John 15:5 (branch/vine/fruit)

- Psalm 1:3 (leaf)
- 2 Corinthians 12:7 (thorn)
- 1 Peter 3:21 (dirt)
- Isaiah 28:27 (stick)
- Proverbs 6:6 (ant)
- John 4:14 (water)

Let's Talk

Look at the things in your collection bag. What are some ways we can take care of these things that God made? Why do you think He gave man the responsibility of caring for His creation?

FOOD CREATION MENAGERIE

Scripture:

Then God said, "Let us make mankind in our image, in our likeness, so that they may rule over the fish in the sea and the birds in the sky, over the livestock and all the wild animals, and over all the creatures that move along the ground" (Genesis 1:26, NIV).

Supplies Needed:

- an assortment of small pieces of fruits, vegetables, cheese, bread (grapes, cherry tomatoes, cheese cubes, bread cubes, celery, baby carrots, olives, broccoli, cauliflower, lettuce, apple cubes, slice of banana, raisins…)
- toothpicks (could be broken in half) and/or small wooden skewers
- bowls
- waxed paper

Let's Talk

Read Genesis 1:26 together. *Earth Day was set aside as a day when we remember that we should take care of our planet in every way. How can we do that? It is important to remember to take care of the plants, animals, forests, and rivers, BUT it is more important to remember WHY we take care of everything on our planet and WHO it really belongs to. Why are we supposed to take care of the fish and the birds and the animals and the planet? Because that's one of the jobs God gave man—His creation. God has the right to give us those marching orders because of WHO He is. Who is He? He's the One who made everything in the first place! All creation belongs to Him. We belong to Him, so He gets to tell us what His plans are for us, and one of those plans is to care for what He created.*

Activity

Give each kid a piece of waxed paper and some toothpicks and/or skewers. They will also need access to the wide variety of foods that you have put together. The more foods you have, the more fun this is. Assign children certain foods to bring in, and they only need to bring a little if you have a large variety. One cubed apple would be enough and one small bunch of grapes or a little box of raisins. Part of the fun is using a bunch of different foods, and only a little of each is needed.

The kids will assemble any of the creations listed in the Bible verse: man, fish, birds, animals, or creatures that move across the ground. Depending on the amount of time you have, they may be able to make more than one. Create a crazy food menagerie! Give the kids time to share what they made and to look at all the others.

Thank God for all He created. Pray that each child will do a good job as a caretaker of God's creation.

PICNIC PROJECT

Scriptures:

It is a land the Lord your God cares for; the eyes of the Lord your God are continually on it from the beginning of the year to its end (Deuteronomy 11:12, NIV).

For we are God's handiwork, created in Christ Jesus to do good works, which God prepared in advance for us to do (Ephesians 2:10, NIV).

Supplies Needed:

- picnic lunches
- blankets
- disposable gloves
- large garbage bags
- sanitary wipes
- camera
- Bibles

Activity

Beforehand, scout out a place where you could have a picnic, but choose a place that is also in need of some attention. More than likely this isn't going to be a picnic area at a public park. It may be along a waterway or in a vacant lot. Seriously, you can have a picnic just about anywhere! You can either have the kids bring a picnic lunch, or you can provide one for them. Spread out some blankets and eat your lunch on the ground.

Once the kids have finished their lunches, pass out disposable gloves and some large garbage bags. The first thing they'll put in their bags is their lunch garbage. Take photos of the kids up against some of the trashier areas of your chosen location, specifically the place that a child (or small group of kids) has chosen to tackle as their clean up project.

Now it's time to get to work! Go at it with a vengeance, having the kids pick up every disgusting thing they come across. Once the area is clean, take the same picture pose as before to show what the area looks like after the kids put some muscle into it.

Let's Talk

Go back to the picnic blankets and read Deuteronomy 11:12 together. *How does God feel about the Earth He created? How can you tell that He cares for it? He always has His eye on His creation—that's us and everything else He spoke into being. He keeps His eye on His creation because He loves us so very much. Remember that when He created each day, His response was, "It is good!"*

Now read Ephesians 2:10 together. *According to this verse, what are we created to do? We're supposed to do good works. How did you feel when we first started this project? Did it feel like too big a job to handle? How did you feel when we took those second photos? We don't do projects like this just to make a field look prettier so property will be worth more money! As people who believe in and follow the One True God, we do this good deed out of respect for the God who made everything. Can you look around today and say, "It is good"?*

Earth Day, April 22, is the largest civic event in the world where countries simultaneously focus on taking care of the Earth. It is not a federal holiday, and no one gets Earth Day off from work. The first one was in 1970, initiated by Senator Nelson from Wisconsin, who had been greatly impacted by seeing the results of an oil spill off the coast of California. Since that time, Earth Day has grown in popularity and has been used to spearhead many environmental changes. These changes have helped us respect and care for what God created. He appointed us as the Earth's caretakers. ("Earth Day: The History of a Movement")

FLOWER LEGACY

Scripture:

I remember your genuine faith, for you share the faith that first filled your grandmother Lois and your mother, Eunice. And I know that same faith continues strong in you (2 Timothy 1:5, NLT).

Supplies Needed:

- random artificial flowers
- green construction paper
- scissors
- black markers
- white glue
- hot glue gun and glue
- branch from a tree
- large pot
- sand and gravel

Let's Talk

Read 2 Timothy 1:5 together. *Timothy's mother was Eunice, and his grandmother was Lois. Both of these women had shared their faith with Timothy and taught him about God. What happened as a result of that? Check out the end of the verse. The result was that Timothy's faith in God was strong.*

It helps when we have people around us who are teaching us to follow God. We can watch how they live and know how we should live. We can watch their habits of reading the Bible, being kind to others, and praying. Then we'll want to read the Bible, be kind, and pray. There are some women whom I've looked to in my life to help me know God better. This would be a wonderful time to tell about how one or two of these women impacted your life.

Activity

Since it's Mother's Day, we're going to think about the women in our lives who help us grow closer to God. Do you know what a legacy is? A legacy is what people remember about you when you're no longer here on Earth. What do you want people to remember about you? I want them to remember that I walked with God each day and did my best to follow His Word.

Beforehand, mount a large bare branch in a large pot filled with sand and gravel. The kids will make a Flowering Legacy Branch. Provide a variety of artificial flowers, already clipped from their stems. The kids will make a large leaf from green construction paper and cut it out. On the leaf they will write (using a black marker) the name of a woman who teaches them about God through words and/or actions. Encourage them to write the name, and not "Mom" or "Grandma." They will use white glue to attach their leaf to the artificial flower they choose. Then an adult will hot glue the flower and leaf onto the branch in a spot the child chooses.

Each of these flowers represents someone special who leads you to God. Place the Flowering Legacy Branch in a place where people can read the names written on the leaves.

HATS OFF TO MOMS

Scripture:

Her children rise up and call her blessed
(Proverbs 31:28, ESV).

Supplies Needed:

- a variety of hats
- video camera

Let's Talk

Read Proverbs 31:28 together. *The Bible tells us that God wants mothers to live in such a way that their children will "rise up and call her blessed." That means following God in everything they do—whether that is for themselves, for a friend, for a stranger, for their spouse, or for their kids. A mom's children will honor her and thank her for all that she does. Her children will not just sit back and take it all for granted, but will rise up. They will do something that recognizes her desire is to follow God in raising her kids. Let's rise up and bless our moms today!*

Activity

Would you like to do a little something special for moms for Mother's Day but want to steer away from making a craft or a card? Round up a variety of hats and get out the video camera. The kids will have a blast making up their own sayings to go along with the hats and then putting those hats on to record their messages. Make copies of the hat tribute as a gift to moms. Now that's an awesome, hat-astic gift!

Here are some ideas to get you started:

TO ALL THE WOMEN IN OUR LIVES, WE WANT TO SAY...

Army Helmet
Thanks for going to battle for us and defending us.

Coonskin Hat
Thanks for going where no one has gone before on our behalf, trying things you never thought you'd try.

Cowboy Hat
Thanks for rounding up our friends, so we can have a great time together.

Birthday Cake Hat
Thanks for helping us celebrate our special day!

Construction Hat
Thanks for working so hard and for all the times you've had tired muscles on our account.

Baker Hat
Thanks for making sure we get fed and for all the cupcakes and cookies—even when they came from the grocery store.

Welder Hat
Thanks for welding us together as a family.

Camouflage Hat
Thanks for everything you do that goes unnoticed.

Toucan Hat
(Yes, I have a hat that looks like a toucan with a giant beak!) Thanks for being nosy and keeping us out of trouble.

Top Hat
Lastly, we want to say, "You're the tops!"

Hats off to YOU!

How about...?

- Park ranger hat
- Pirate hat
- Indian headdress

- Fireman's hat
- Police officer's hat
- Sombrero
- Crown
- Turban
- Alpine hat
- Viking hat
- Pilgrim hat
- Sherlock Holmes' hat
- Jester hat
- Railroad engineer's hat
- Football helmet

MAKE MOM LAUGH

Scriptures:

A cheerful heart is good medicine
(Proverbs 17:22a, NLT).

She is clothed with strength and dignity, and she laughs without fear of the future
(Proverbs 31:25, NLT).

Supplies Needed:

- camera
- photo paper
- scissors
- laminator
- ribbon
- hot glue

Let's Talk

What makes your mom laugh? Sometimes it's silly things you do. Sometimes she's excited about something. Maybe it's a scene in a movie you're watching together. How does it make you feel to hear your mom laugh?

Let's see what the Bible says about laughing. Read Proverbs 17:22a. *It sure sounds to me like laughter is good for you! Although the research has not been done, many doctors agree that people who laugh a lot are healthier and are able to deal with their illnesses better.*

Read Proverbs 31:25. *The entire chapter of Proverbs 31 talks about what a godly woman is like. In this verse it says that a godly woman laughs at what? She can look at the future, no matter what she thinks might happen, and laugh…or at least smile…because she knows she's not alone. God is always with her, and that means she doesn't have to be afraid.*

Activity

Take individual pictures of the kids in crazy poses, making funny faces. Get as little background as possible in the photos. Print these out on photo paper or card stock. The kids will very carefully cut themselves out, being as detailed as possible. Once the picture is cut out, then laminate it and trim around the picture, leaving about ¼" of the lamination. Use a hot glue gun to attach a piece of ribbon. *Now you've got a crazy bookmark to give Mom. Every time she opens her book and sees your funny pose, it will bring a smile to her face.*

STAINED GLASS HEART

Scripture:

But Mary treasured up all these things and pondered them in her heart (Luke 2:19, NIV).

Supplies Needed:

- heart cookie cutters
- sugar
- measuring cups and spoons
- white corn syrup
- cream of tartar
- candy thermometer
- food coloring
- saucepan
- cooking spray
- foil
- cookie sheet
- craft sticks

Instructions:

- Cover a cookie sheet with foil and spray the foil with nonstick cooking spray. Spray the inside of some heart-shaped cookie cutters also, and set them on the cookie sheet.
- In a saucepan combine 1¾ c. sugar, ½ c. white corn syrup, 1 c. water, and 1/8 t. cream of tartar.
- Heat this mixture on the stove slowly until it comes to a low boil, all the while continuously stirring.
- Set a candy thermometer in the mixture and continue stirring on the low boil until the thermometer reads 300°.
- Ladle the mixture into the cookie cutters. Some may seep out under the cookie cutter, but don't be too concerned with that. Do your best to keep the cookie cutter pressed against the cookie sheet while pouring.
- Drop a few drops of food coloring into the hearts. Drag a craft stick gently through the drops and the mixture to make swirls of color. Be careful not to bump the cookie cutter.
- Do not move the cookie sheet. Leave it there until the sugar mixture hardens. When you can tell that it is getting solid, you can carefully move the cookie sheet to the refrigerator to speed up the cooling process.
- Carefully remove the sugar hearts from the cookie cutters.

Let's Talk

Read Luke 2:19. *The Bible tells us that when Mary gave birth to Jesus, she filed away in her heart the memories of all that happened. What do you think she remembered for years to come? She probably could recall the frustration of not being able to find a place to lie down that night. I bet she could remember Jesus' little hands wrapped around her finger and the tiny little sounds He made. She probably remembered wrapping the cloth around Him, hugging Him close, and then watching Him in the manger all night long. She probably could remember the looks on the shepherds' faces as they entered the stable, and still could hear the proud voice of Joseph. All these things were memories no one could take away from her.*

Moms are like that! So many things that happen seem so ordinary to us, but to mothers they are special. Moms treasure those moments and keep them in their hearts and minds for the rest of their lives. When they ponder them, they can be right back there experiencing the moment with you all over again. What kind of things do you think your mom remembers and treasures about you? Do you think she remembers the day you took your first step, or when you lost your first tooth, or that first ride on your bike without training wheels, or how you spent so much time making a card just for her? Oh yeah, she remembers! That's because you are so very special to her.

Give the swirled stained-glass heart to your mom. Ask her to share some things she remembers... some things she pondered...when you were just a baby.

CLOUD OF WITNESSES POSTER

Scripture:

Therefore, since we are surrounded by such a great cloud of witnesses, let us throw off everything that hinders and the sin that so easily entangles. And let us run with perseverance the race marked out for us (Hebrews 12:1, NIV).

Supplies Needed:

- white poster board
- cotton balls
- pencils
- scissors
- glue
- markers

Let's Talk

Read Hebrews 12:1 together. *On this Memorial Day we can think about a great cloud of witnesses as being the people who died in battle for the freedom of this country. We are "surrounded" by them in a way, since we are benefiting from what they sacrificed. If it weren't for them, we would not be sitting here today without fear of being arrested or worse.*

The "great cloud of witnesses" could also be people who have died because they were Christ-followers—preaching and meeting together in the name of Christ. This isn't just something that happened a long time ago. It happens each and every day all over our world.

> *In 2013, the annual study on Christian martyrs done by Open Doors Ministry reported to Reuters News Agency that they had documented over 2,100 "martyr" killings that year, almost twice as many as the year before (Heneghan).*

The other thing this "great cloud of witnesses" could be is the people right now who are giving their lives, their time, and resources to be a godly example to others. They are rooting for new believers, and they're rooting for those who are thinking about making that decision, and they are rooting for those who don't even know who Jesus is yet. They're like God's cheerleading team! They listen. They answer questions. They share their lives with people who want to know more about Jesus and how He can change their lives for eternity.

Who do you look to as a godly example? Who do you go to with questions about God? Who do you watch to see how they handle tough situations? Who is part of your cloud of witnesses?

The purpose of Memorial Day is to honor those who died defending our country. How can you best honor your cloud of witnesses? The best way I know is to live to honor God the way they did and always chase after God with your whole heart. Then you'll become the cloud of witnesses for others.

Activity

Give each child a half sheet of white poster board. The kids will sketch with a pencil the outline of a cloud (as close to the size of the poster board as possible). Cut this out. Then, using all different colors of markers and writing styles, put the names of people who support you and lead you to God. They should make a caption, something like: "My Cloud of Witnesses".

Once they have that done, then they can outline their cloud by gluing cotton balls around the edge. They may also want to fill in some of the middle between the names.

Pray and thank God for each of the people listed on these posters.

FLUSH IT!

Scripture:

For I will forgive their wickedness and will remember their sins no more
(Hebrews 8:12, NIV).

Supplies Needed:

- toilet paper
- ballpoint pens
- toilet

Let's Talk

Memorial Day is all about remembering—remembering what fallen soldiers sacrificed for our country. But did you know that there is something God can't remember? Now you're saying, "I thought God could do everything." And He can. Can you "not remember" on purpose? Can you decide you're not going to remember something mean that happened to you? You can try, but it's always there. God's the only One who can "not remember" when He chooses to.

So, what is it that God does not remember? When we claim Jesus as our Savior and say, "I disobeyed God, but I believe Jesus is the Son of God and took my punishment for all I've done wrong," the Bible tells us that God will forget those sins. He doesn't just forgive them; He forgets them! Read Hebrews 8:12. *He's not going to bring your sin back up again. He's done with it because He has the power to forget when He wants to. That's amazing! And, boy, am I glad He can do that because I can't forget how I disobeyed Him. It's always back there in my memory.*

Activity

Give the kids a piece of toilet paper (a couple of squares). You want a fairly strong brand, not the cheapest stuff. Using a ballpoint pen, the kids will write ways they have disobeyed God on their squares of toilet paper. If they have asked God to forgive those sins, then God has forgotten them. *Our sins are nasty in the sight of God. He doesn't want them hanging around, so He forgets them. God doesn't want to even be in the presence of the remembrance of a sin.*

Take the kids to a bathroom where they can gather around a toilet. Yes, they're going to kind of get weird on you for a moment, and let them. Then reign them back in and move on. *If you have asked for forgiveness for this nastiness in your life, then throw your toilet paper into the toilet. Let's give them a big old flush! Those sins are gone, and God's not going to try to fetch them out of the toilet!*

RED POPPY

Scripture:

And when He had taken some bread and given thanks, He broke it and gave it to them, saying, "This is My body which is given for you; do this in remembrance of Me." And in the same way He took the cup after they had eaten, saying, "This cup which is poured out for you is the new covenant in My blood" (Luke 22:19-20, NASB).

Supplies Needed:

- green chenille sticks
- red paper cupcake liners (any size)
- scissors
- black marker
- tiny yellow pom-poms
- school glue
- hot glue gun

Let's Talk

In 1918, as she thought about what Memorial Day meant, Moina Michael wrote these words in a poem:

We cherish, too, the Poppy red
That grows on fields where valor led;
It seems to signal to the skies
That blood of heroes never dies....
(Excerpt from "We Shall Keep the Faith")

These words launched a national tradition of wearing a red poppy on Memorial Day. Many times you will see veterans distributing them outside of stores. When you see the poppy, it reminds you of the people who have shed blood and died to protect our country.

As Christians, we have been protected for eternity because of blood that was shed and the One who died for us. His name is Jesus—the very Son of God, who was perfect and did not deserve to be punished. It was a different kind of battlefield that He fought on—a cross and then a grave. But He came out of that battle with the "win."

Read together Luke 22:19-20. *Jesus said these words as He shared His last meal with His disciples...right before heading to the cross. Every time we eat bread or take a drink, He wants us to remember Him. We do this at special times called Communion, but really any time we eat or drink, we should pause and remember...and have a Memorial Day for Jesus. Why would Jesus want us to remember Him? Because when we admit our sins that demand the punishment of being forever separated from God, and accept that Jesus took our punishment for us, then we need to thank Him constantly for saving our lives—our eternal, forever lives. It's because of Him that we are brought back to God and will live forever with Him. It's because of His sacrifice that we can have the Holy Spirit helping us live each day.*

Activity

- Give each child 2 red cupcake liners. On one of them, the kids will barely cut the top edge off, making it curve in and out. On the second liner, they will make the same curved cut, but about halfway down the side of the liner.
- Use a black permanent marker to make lines out from the center with dots on the ends. It should resemble a fireworks explosion.
- Place a dot of school glue in the center of the larger liner. Then place the smaller liner (with the black center) on top of it. This will give 2 layers to the flower petals.

- Glue a small yellow pom-pom in the center of the black area.
- An adult will use a hot glue gun to attach a green chenille stick to the back of the flower to make the stem.

Place your poppy somewhere to remind you not only of the soldiers who died for our country, but of Jesus, our Savior, who died to protect us from Satan for all eternity.

STONES OF REMEMBRANCE

Scripture:

Joshua set up the twelve stones that had been in the middle of the Jordan at the spot where the priests who carried the ark of the covenant had stood. And they are there to this day (Joshua 4:9, NIV).

Supplies Needed:

- 12 good-sized stones or bricks
- Two 8-foot boards

Let's Talk

Have you ever been to a military cemetery? Rows and rows of white stone crosses represent the soldiers who have died for our country. Those stones remind us of what those men did. On Memorial Day we pause to remember them—in fact, at 3:00 p.m. wherever you are, you are supposed to observe one minute of silence.

In the fourth chapter of Joshua, the Bible talks about a special stone memorial too. The Israelites had been wandering around the desert for 40 years and were now ready to head into the Promised Land and take the city of Jericho. The Jordan River was in the way, though, and it was flooded. God told Joshua to have the priests pick up the Ark of the Covenant and walk to the river. When they stepped into the water, God caused the river to part and make a path of dry land.

Joshua instructed one person from each of the 12 tribes to pick up a stone from the dry riverbed as they walked across and to take those stones to the other side. Can you count to 12? Now count backwards from 12! Anyway…back to the story. In their camp at Gilgal, they used those 12 stones to build a memorial. Anytime future generations saw that pile of stones, they would remember how God brought the Israelites into the Promised Land.

Joshua also took 12 stones and put them in a pile right in the middle of the riverbed. Yep, right there as the floodwaters were waiting to come crashing down again. It was a memorial also. When the priests made it to the other side with the Ark and stepped onto the shore, immediately the floodwaters came rushing back down and covered the stones. But every time the waters receded from the flood stage, the rocks would show up and remind the people how God pulled back the water so they could cross.

Build a Memorial

Lay 2 8-foot boards parallel on the ground, about 12"-18" apart. Place 12 large stones (or you could use bricks) in between these boards in various places. (If you're using stones, make sure you get larger ones, not just little pocket-sized rocks.) Mark a place away from the boards where the stones should be carried. This will be determined according to the size of the stones and the age of your kids.

We're going to cross the Jordan River and pick up a stone, just like the Israelites did! The kids will walk across the boards, with their right foot on the right board and their left foot on the left board. At some point as they cross, they will pick up one of the stones that is in between the boards and carry it to the designated spot. *This spot is where the Israelites camped. Use the stones to build a memorial in that place.*

Is there anything, when you see it, that reminds you of God and something He has done in your life or in someone else's life?

Memorial Day is a day for remembering those who have died fighting for our country. Originally known as Decoration Day, individual northern states started honoring their dead after the Civil War by decorating their graves. Southern states did not join in the special day of observance until after World War I, when the day changed from just honoring the deceased from the Civil War to include those who had fallen in any war. At this time people started calling the day Memorial Day, but the name wasn't officially changed until legislation was signed in 1967.

CARRY ME

Scriptures:

Then I said to you, "Do not be terrified; do not be afraid of them. The Lord your God, who is going before you, will fight for you, as he did for you in Egypt, before your very eyes, and in the wilderness. There you saw how the Lord your God carried you, as a father carries his son, all the way you went until you reached this place" (Deuteronomy 1:29-31, NIV).

He tends his flock like a shepherd: He gathers the lambs in his arms and carries them close to his heart; he gently leads those that have young (Isaiah 40:11, NIV).

Supplies Needed:

- old shirt (size 4 or larger)
- old pants (size 4 or larger)
- stuffing–newspaper, quilt batting, shipping air pillows
- large safety pins
- 3 traffic cones for each group

Let's Talk

Read both Deuteronomy 1:29-31 and Isaiah 40:11. *What do these two scriptures have in common? Is there something that is mentioned in both of them? Both of them talk about God "carrying" us. Has your dad ever carried you? When did that happen? Was it a piggyback ride? Were you playing horsey on the floor? Were you hurt and he carried you to a place where you could be taken care of? Were you asleep in the car and he carried you into the house? Have you ever looked up at your dad when you're tired and said, "Carry me"? Dads are bigger and stronger than we are, and they can carry their kids. It's always a good thing when Dad carries you.*

God is our Heavenly Dad. He's even more powerful and stronger than your dad here on earth. The Bible says He will carry you. He doesn't want to carry just your problems. He wants to carry you! He wants to take care of you, love you, and hold you close. He wants to carry you when you're hurt and when you're tired, but also when you're having fun with your friends. Can you imagine what it looks like for God to carry you? What does that feel like? When do you know that God is carrying you?

Activity

Each group of 4-6 kids will need an old shirt, an old pair of pants, some stuffing, and a supply of safety pins. The stuffing can be newspapers, quilt batting, or shipping air pillows. The kids will then pin the ends of the shirt sleeves and the neck closed. Now stuff the shirt. They will do the same with the pants, pinning the cuffs first. Then they will pin the shirt and pants together to make the body of a person. They may want to add a brown paper bag head also. But all you really need for the activity is the main body.

Determine a starting point and an ending point. In between, randomly place 3 traffic cones. The kids will take turns putting their stuffed person on their back, pulling the arms together around their neck so they can keep "him" there. They will carry their person to the ending point, weaving in and out of the 3 traffic cones as they go. Depending on your kids' level of understanding, when they reach the ending point, they will either say:

- "God, my Heavenly Dad, wants to carry me."
- OR they can tell the leader a time when they recognized God carrying them.

Return the stuffed person to the starting point so the next person can carry him.

GAME SHOW GOLF

Scripture:

He will turn the hearts of fathers to their children and the hearts of children to their fathers (Malachi 4:6a, ESV).

Supplies Needed:

- cardboard box
- box cutter
- golf balls
- putters (real or play)
- assorted candy bars (as chosen)
- paper
- markers
- tape

Let's Talk

Read Malachi 4:6a together. *What does this verse say to you? Fathers need to pay attention to their children, and children need to pay attention to their fathers. Fathers should love their kids, and kids should love their dads. A father's heart should want the very best for his child, and that includes the #1 thing—that his child walks with God all the days of his/her life. It means that a child's heart should want the very best for his/her dad, and that includes that he makes God #1 in his life every single day.*

One of the things we can do to bring people closer together is to play together. Many times we play separately, but we don't play together. Our hearts grow closer when we play, but kids' games and grown-up games don't always match up. We've got one that will, though! And not only will you play together, but you'll also be able to tell your dad, in kind of a funny way, how special he is as the game is played.

Game

To make the game, use a box cutter (an adult does this) to cut some arches out of one side of a cardboard box. These are going to be the holes that you'll try to putt the golf balls into during the game. Make at least 3 down one side of the box, but do as many as you can (depends on the size of the box). Make a sign for the top of the box that says "Game Show Golf."

Also, the kids should prepare some prize candy bars with silly but uplifting sayings written on pieces of paper and taped to the candy bar.

- **PayDay** – You deserve an extra PayDay, Dad!
- **100 Grand** – I'd love to give you 100 Grand for Father's Day.
- **Mounds** – I appreciate all that you do, Mounds and Mounds.
- **Skor** – You Skor big when it comes to being a dad.
- **Zero** – There are Zero dads better than you.
- **Uno** – You are numero Uno, number 1, in my book.
- **Take Five** – You deserve to Take Five and get a little rest.

The kid will be the game show host, but also a player. As the game show host, he/she will say, "Welcome to Game Show Golf, where dads are always like a hole in one—the best there is."

This can be played outside or inside. If inside, play with a plastic toy putter (or make a putter from a 3' piece of PVC pipe, an "L" joint, and a shorter piece of PVC—5"). Position the box at a fair distance so that the holes are facing the players. Dad and kid(s), in that order, will take turns putting their golf ball at the holes. Each time Dad gets a ball into a hole, give him one of the candy bars. As it is presented to him, read what is written on the candy bar in a game show voice.

Have fun and turn your hearts toward one another!

HONOR WITH ART

Scripture:

Honor your father and your mother, so that you may live long in the land the Lord your God is giving you (Exodus 20:12, NIV).

Supplies Needed:

- white card stock half-sheets
- drawing supplies
- stapler

Let's Talk

Read together Exodus 20:12. *What does this verse tell us to do for our fathers? We are to honor them. What does honor mean? It means to show respect. It means to make them feel good about what they do. It means not to be ashamed of them when talking to others. It means remembering and pointing out the good things they do and are.*

This verse is a commandment. It's not a suggestion like, "If you feel like it today, you can honor your dad." It's also a commandment with a promise. Life will be better when we honor our fathers, even if they've done something to hurt our feelings or done things we don't understand. God tells us to honor them, and it will be good for us. You will have a clear heart, knowing you have obeyed your Heavenly Father.

We're going to honor our dads (or significant male figure if the child does not have a father) through drawing.

Activity

The kids will draw a book that honors their father. Give each child a set of 6-8 half-sheets of white card stock. They will draw a picture that depicts each one of these things on separate pieces of card stock. Do not draw on the 1-inch margin at the left end of the paper. That's where all the pages will be stapled when the drawings are completed.

Make a front cover that says something like, "I Honor You, Dad!"

Draw pictures that depict:

- What you most like to do with your dad.
- What your dad said that made you laugh. Draw a cartoon with conversation balloons.
- Your dad's favorite food.
- Your favorite place to go with your dad.
- If your dad were a superhero, which one would he be? Draw a picture of your dad as a superhero. You can even make up a new one!
- A gift you would like to give your dad if you could give him anything.

SANDING DISCIPLINE

Scriptures:

My son, do not despise the Lord's discipline, and do not resent his rebuke, because the Lord disciplines those he loves, as a father the son he delights in (Proverbs 3:11-12, NIV).

He disciplines us for our good, that we may share his holiness (Hebrews 12:10b, ESV).

Supplies Needed:

- scrap pieces of wood
- sandpaper
- black permanent marker
- power sander

Let's Talk

A cavity is a rotten place in your tooth. What happens when you get a cavity? You have to go to the dentist. What does the dentist do to the cavity? He fills it, but before he does that, he has to sand out the rotten stuff that is there. He's got to get rid of it, so he can make your tooth the way it should be.

One of the responsibilities of dads is to discipline their children. That's really not the part we like, is it? We don't like getting punished or when our dads make us do something that makes our wrongs right—when we have to apologize or fix something. When you get disciplined, it's so you won't do the wrong thing again. You were doing something that was bad for your character or dangerous to you or someone else. Discipline is like getting rid of the rotten stuff in your tooth so the good filling can be put in.

Your dad isn't the only one who disciplines you, though. Your Heavenly Daddy does also. When you go through a difficult time, you think, "Hey, God, why did You let that happen to me?" It's because God is using the experience to discipline you—to bring you closer to His character. Every bad situation has something for you to learn from it.

Why does God have to discipline me? Isn't it enough that my dad does? Read Proverbs 3:11-12. *This verse tells us why God bothers to discipline you. It's because He loves you. He wants you to be the best you possible, and sometimes you need help getting on the right track.* Read Hebrews 12:10. *Why else does God discipline you? This verse says that it's for your own good! You know what? God created you, and because He created you, He knows what's best for you. Because He's the best Father there could be, He has to do what is best for you. Let's say "Happy Father's Day" to God…the best Dad ever!*

Activity

Give each child a scrap piece of 2" x 4" or similar kind of board. On the board they will use a marker to write just a few words that describe a tough time they're going through. Be ready, because these could be anything from "Housebreaking my dog" to "Parents getting a divorce." *When we go through tough times, God uses them to sand us, to make us smoother, to make us into someone more like Him.* The kids will use a piece of sandpaper to sand over what they have written until the writing is gone. *That's a lot of work, and it took a while to do. Sometimes it takes a long time to get through a tough situation and learn all the lessons that we can from it. We just keep focused on God during that time, thinking about what He would want us to do, praying for His guidance, and reading His Word for help.*

Get out the power sander. Run it over one of the blocks that has something written on it. The words will sand down a lot faster. *Sometimes we get through our tough time really quickly, just like how fast this sander got rid of the words. But, even if it doesn't last long, God can discipline us through that.*

What have you learned from going through something difficult?

When our country celebrates its freedom on July 4th, what do we do to make that celebration special? Fireworks! Where do you usually see fireworks? They're always outside. Well…maybe not always, because we're going to show you how to have indoor fireworks that are a blast! We're going to have some crazy fireworks without lighting a match and without using a firecracker.

Activity

This activity is going to get loud, so be prepared! Give half of the kids the celebration statement, "Jesus is the truth!" and the other half the celebration statement, "The truth sets you free!" Lay pieces of bubble wrap all over the floor. The big bubbled bubble wrap works best, or you can use the air packing pillows.

The leader will hold a live microphone down close to the bubble wrap. If you have a large group, then have several live microphones ready. At the leader's signal, the kids will jump on the bubble wrap. Each time they pop the bubble wrap, they should YELL their celebration statement. The microphone will increase the volume of the popping and make it sound like fireworks.

FIREWORKS

Scripture:

You will know the truth, and the truth will set you free (John 8:32, NIV).

Supplies Needed:

- handheld microphone
- bubble wrap with the large bubbles

Let's Talk

The United States celebrates the 4th of July in remembrance of being set free from England. It's a day of freedom! As Christians, we have an even better freedom, and it doesn't matter what country we live in. We have the freedom Jesus gives us, and that is freedom from our sin. Because Jesus is the truth of God, when we believe in the Truth, everything that has hold of us—all our sins—just don't stand a chance. We've been set free from them because Jesus took the punishment that was really ours. Read John 8:32. *The Bible can't get much clearer than that!*

When a prisoner is set free from jail, it's because he has paid for his crime by spending time in jail—his punishment. Jesus paid for our crimes—our sins—by taking the punishment of dying on the cross. So we can be free!

FREEDOM TO SERVE

Scripture:

For you have been called to live in freedom, my brothers and sisters. But don't use your freedom to satisfy your sinful nature. Instead, use your freedom to serve one another in love (Galatians 5:13, NLT).

Supplies Needed:

- cardboard toilet paper rolls
- ingredients for trail mix

- scissors
- poster board
- red, white, and blue craft paints
- paintbrushes
- pencil
- tape
- snack bags
- hot glue
- patterned scrapbooking paper
- silver chenille sticks
- labels

Instructions:

- Set the toilet paper roll against a piece of poster board and use the end as a pattern to make a circle. Cut this circle out as precisely as possible. An adult will put some hot glue along the bottom edge of the toilet paper roll and adhere this circle to close one end of the tube. Once the glue is completely dry, you can move on. (An adult may want to have this step done before the activity begins.)
- Give the kids red, white, and blue paints to decorate their tubes. Set them aside to dry.
- Draw a 3½" circle on the underside of a piece of red, white, and blue patterned scrapbooking paper. (A can of icing is the perfect size to use as a stencil to draw around!) Cut this out and set aside.
- The kids will need to fill a snack-sized baggie with trail mix. The kids can make this themselves (choosing their favorite ingredients to include in their bag) or use a prepackaged snack mix.
- Once the paint is dry, it's time to assemble. Put the snack bag inside the tube.
- A leader will run a bead of hot glue around the top edge, and then the kids will cover the open end with the patterned paper circle, leaving a skirt around the edges.
- Cut a piece of silver chenille stick about 3" long and coil it around a pencil. Gently poke one end through the center of the paper. This makes the lit wick.
- Add a preprinted sticker. It could say: "There's freedom in Jesus." Include your church name if you like.

Let's Talk

Read Galatians 5:13. *Christ gives us a freedom that not even our great country can offer us. If you have asked God to forgive you and have turned yourself over to what He wants for your life, then you are free for eternity...forever. Out of gratitude, what does this verse say we should do with our freedom? Show it to others by the way we serve them.*

Have your kids make a bunch of these to give away—paint them and put them together in an assembly line. Challenge them to think of some people they could give them to. Maybe they could take them to the homeless shelter where people are standing in line for their daily meal or pass them out at the community parade. What if you stood outside a grocery store or even the fireworks stand and presented them to passersby...with a big smile on your face!

SECRET WORSHIP

Scripture:

Now the Lord is the Spirit, and where the Spirit of the Lord is, there is freedom
(2 Corinthians 3:17, ESV).

Supplies Needed:

- candle

Locate a room that can be darkened and has a clear corner big enough for all the kids to fit in. Take the kids to this place for worship time. They should huddle together as close as possible. Turn the lights down and light a small candle, placing it where the kids won't be tempted to blow into or reach for it.

Sing a couple of worship songs a cappella.

Let's Talk

Is this how we usually worship? How is this different from the way we usually sing and praise God together?

One of the beautiful things about the freedom in our country—the freedom we celebrate on the 4th of July—is that we can gather and worship God without being afraid of someone throwing us in jail or even killing us for coming together. We don't have to be frightened. Being able to worship the way we want is one of the main reasons our country was started in the first place. Freedom to worship is a very precious right that we have because we live in this country.

There are people all over the world who wish they could worship God out in the open, but they can't. If they want to worship together, they have to hide in a dark corner of a secret place, kind of like we have done here today. They sing softly, so no one will hear them outside.

- *How would that make you feel?*
- *Would you be frightened?*
- *Why do you think people in other parts of the world worship in secret, even when it's against the law?*
- *What do you think they would say to us?*

Close your time in the darkened room by praying together. Thank God for the freedom we have to worship without fear. Also pray diligently for those people who worship God even though their lives may be threatened for doing so. Pray that God will make a way for them and keep them strong in their faith.

UNTANGLED FREEDOM

Scripture:

Jesus spoke to the Jews who had believed him. "If you obey my teaching," he said, "you are really my disciples. Then you will know the truth. And the truth will set you free" (John 8:31-32, NIrV).

Supplies Needed:

- old sheets cut into 4" wide, long strips
- bread
- soft margarine
- jelly
- dessert paper plates
- plastic knives

Activity

Using the long pieces of sheeting, tie the children together in groups of four. Tie one ankle from each of two children together and one wrist of two other children. Continue tying the four kids together in a confusing mess. Avoid keeping them in a straight line. Experiment with making one child cross his/her legs and another hold one hand behind his/her back. This becomes quite a tangle.

Now that they are tangled, the task of each group is to make one sandwich, using a piece of bread spread with margarine and topped with some jelly. Once the sandwich is completed, untie the children and take note of their comments as they are being released.

Let's Talk

Repeat some of the comments you heard as the kids were being untied after the exercise.

We celebrate the 4th of July as a day to remember when this new country was set free from Great Britain, the country that considered the people of America as property they owned and controlled.

How do you think the people of America felt on that day, when they found out they were no longer property of Great Britain? Freedom feels so much better when you've known what it's like not to be free to live like you want to live.

How was this tangled exercise like our lives when we let Satan hold us in sin? Sin confuses our lives and causes us to live with a lot of guilt. The messes we've gotten into and the things we've not admitted to keep coming to mind. What have you done that made you feel guilty?

- *How did it feel to be untied? Did you appreciate your freedom more than you did before the exercise?*
- *How did you feel toward the person who untied you?*
- *How does it feel when you admit how you've done wrong and don't have to feel guilty any longer?*

Everything in the Bible tells us the truth that comes from God. He's the One who created us, so He knows what's best for His creation. He knows the TRUTH about what will set us free. The Bible tells us that because of Jesus rescuing us we don't have to be held tight by our sins. When you declare your belief in Jesus, claim His sacrifice that will pay for the sin in your life, and commit to following Him from that day on, you can be FREE from the sin and the guilt that are holding on to you.

How do you feel toward God—the One who set you free, who untied you when you were caught by your sin?

Read John 8:31-32. Now, shout…really shout… verse 32—*You will know the truth. And the truth will set you free!*

Random Fun Facts

- How many hot dogs do Americans eat on the 4th of July? According to the National Hot Dog and Sausage Council, Americans eat 155 million hot dogs over the 4th of July weekend ("Infoplease Article").
- Congress declared the Fourth of July an official holiday in 1870.
- In 1954 the words "one nation under God" were added to the Pledge of Allegiance.
- On July 2, 1776, in anticipation of the signing of the Declaration of Independence, John Adams wrote these words to his wife, Abigail.

  "The Second Day of July 1776, will be the most memorable Epocha, in the History of America… It ought to be solemnized with Pomp and Parade, with Shews, Games, Sports, Guns, Bells, Bonfires and Illuminations from one End of this Continent to the other, from this Time forward forever more" (DeCosta-Klipa).

  Illuminations? Sounds like fireworks to me!

GROWING ICE

Scripture:

So whether you eat or drink or whatever you do, do it all for the glory of God
(1 Corinthians 10:31, NIV).

Supplies Needed:

- full 16 oz. bottle of water
- food coloring
- clear cup with a wide top
- ice
- pan

Instructions:

- Put a couple of drops of food coloring in a full, 16 oz. bottle of water and seal it tightly.
- Lay the bottle flat on its side in the freezer. Leave it there for 2 hours and 45 minutes. You may have to test this a couple of times to figure out the exact amount of time it will take for your freezer. You want the water to be as cold as it can possibly get without turning to ice.
- In a clear cup, place a mound of ice. Set the cup in a pan that can catch any overflow that might occur.
- Slowly pour the colored water over the ice in the cup. Keep the water coming steadily.
- The water will turn to ice and begin growing like a stalagmite. It's amazing to watch the ice grow upwards.

Let's Talk

Which direction was the ice growing? It was growing upwards. When we talk about God, which way do we point? We point upwards because God is greater than anything; He is above all things and all people.

Read 1 Corinthians 10:31. *How does this verse remind you of our growing ice experiment? Whatever we do…even whatever we drink, like this water…needs to be pleasing to God and bring Him glory. In everything we do, we want to point people upwards toward our great God. How about "whatever we play"? Or "whatever we do for work"? On this Labor Day, we celebrate the work people do, and whatever the work is, it should be done so that God is pleased. It should be done so that God gets glory for it. Our play and our work should be done so that God smiles on it.*

Challenge the kids to name 10 things they do during the week. List these on a dry erase board so you can refer back to them. Go through each one and ask the children to tell how they can please God in that particular thing they are doing. Let's say they said that something they do during the week is play soccer. *How can you please—how can you bring glory to—God when you're playing soccer? The way you react when there is a bad call, when someone gets hurt, when you lose, or when you win will show others whether or not you are living to please God.*

If you don't know whether or not you should do something, what would be a good question to ask yourself? Will this please God? Will God get glory if I do this? If the answer in your heart is "no," what should you do?

Do you want to live by 1 Corinthians 10:31?

HAMMERING HEART

Scripture:

Whatever you do, work at it with all your heart, as working for the Lord, not for human masters (Colossians 3:23, NIV).

Supplies Needed:

- copy of a heart pattern with dots around the outside edge
- tape
- ½" - ¾" thick piece of plywood (6" x 9")
- small hammer
- small nails with large heads
- ball of yarn

Instructions:

- Tape the heart pattern onto the piece of plywood.
- Using a small hammer, the child will tap a nail into each of the dots on the pattern. Make sure the nail is in far enough that it won't come out easily. Continue doing this until each dot has a nail through it.
- Pull the tape off and tear the paper away. Now you have a heart pattern with nails.
- Tie the end of the yarn ball to any of the nails.
- Crisscross in any fashion or pattern, taking the yarn around the nail heads, back and forth. When the child has wrapped as much yarn on as they like, then clip it and tie around the last nail head. You can also change the colors of yarn as you go, tying them off when you have enough of that color.

Let's Talk

Labor Day is about honoring people who do everyday work—the people who build things, teachers, health workers, and those who get food to our tables. They work hard so other people can have a better life. You worked hard at this project, and you were pretty good with your hammering skills. How do you feel about your finished project?

Let's see what the Bible says about working. Read Colossians 3:23. *What is our attitude supposed to be toward the work we do? We're supposed to do our very best and work hard. Sometimes we really like doing the work—hammering these nails into the wood was loads of fun! Name some other times when work is fun. Other times, our work isn't quite so fun, like when you have to pick up stinky garbage. Name some other times when work is not so much fun. Whether it's fun or not, how are we supposed to do it?*

We're supposed to put our whole hearts into it! What do you think that means? When you put your heart into something, you really want it to turn out right…you want to be proud of it…you want to know you didn't give up until it was done.

But this verse says even more than that. It says that no matter who we're working for, we're supposed to do it just as if we're doing it for God. Let's say Jesus was standing right here watching you hammer those nails. Would you want Him to see you doing sloppy work or would you want Him to see how good you could do it? So, when you're working, imagine that Jesus is standing right there and what you're doing is for Him.

KICK IT OVER TO GOD

Scripture:

Commit your works to the Lord And your plans will be established (Proverbs 16:3, NASB).

Supplies Needed:

- 4' pool noodles
- long wooden skewers
- small playground balls
- tape
- paper
- markers
- spray paint
- piece of poster board

Instructions for Game Set-Up:

- You will create 3 wickets for each team. You want as many teams as possible, each with their own set of 3 wickets, so more kids are engaged at the same time. Place the wickets 10-15' apart and not in a straight line. Create the wickets by sticking 2 wooden skewers in the ground about 18" apart. Slide one end of the pool noodle over one skewer. Arch the pool noodle and slide the other end over the other skewer. This is amazingly easy to do and only takes seconds!
- On the grass past the last of the wickets, spray paint in large letters "GOD". This is the goal for each team to reach. Don't worry… the next time the grass is mowed the paint will disappear.
- Also at the destination, place a piece of poster board.

Let's Talk

Read Proverbs 16:3. *What does "commit" mean? When you commit your works to God, you give them over to Him. You put Him in charge of what you're working on, instead of trying to make it work all on your own. This also means that if God wants to move you away from what you have in mind, you're not going to be stubborn about it and you're going to let Him lead you. But that only happens when you commit your works to Him—when you deliver them to Him and hand them over to Him.*

We're celebrating Labor Day and the work people do to earn a living. Adults who are Christ-followers want what they do at their jobs to please God. Committing—handing over—your job to God sounds like, "God, help me to represent You as I sell shoes today. If I get a chance to speak up for You, let me step up and do that." I don't think any of you have a job, so what kind of "works" do you do? (school studies, being part of teams, serving others in big and small ways) *What "works" do you want to commit or hand over to God for Him to use?*

This verse tells us to commit all our works to God. We want to GIVE it over to Him to use as He sees fit. But, in our game today, we're going to KICK it over to Him.

Playing the Game:

- With a marker, the kids will each write on a small piece of paper one "work" they would like to commit to God.
- On their turn, they will put 2 small pieces of tape on the paper (one on each end) and tape the paper to their team's playground ball.

- That player will kick (and this will need to be a stay-on-the-ground kind of kick) the ball so that it goes through their team's first wicket, then the second wicket, and then the third. The goal is to get their ball through all 3 wickets and delivered to the grassy area that says GOD.
- The player will take his/her paper off the ball and say out loud, "I commit ________ to You, God" (filling in the blank with what is on the paper). Then, the player will tape the paper to the poster board that is there.
- The player will grab the ball and run back to his/her team, so the next player can tape a paper on the ball and do the same thing.
- All teams will be aiming for the same goal and using the same piece of poster board.

WORK HARD, BE GENEROUS

Scriptures:

When people work, their wages are not a gift, but something they have earned (Romans 4:4, NLT).

Use your hands for good hard work, and then give generously to others in need (Ephesians 4:28, NLT).

Too often, we give kids the impression that the way they can "earn" money is to stand outside a store with a bucket and ask strangers to give it to them. The Bible teaches something quite different.

Let's Talk

Labor Day is a time when we celebrate everyday people who work hard to make a living. The holiday came about at a time when people worked really, really long hours and never got a day off. Many changes have been made since the first Labor Day, and we now have many more choices for what we can do with the money we earn from jobs. Let's see what the Bible has to say about work.

Read Romans 4:4 together. *What are wages? Wages are the amount of money you are paid if you complete a certain job you were hired to do. If someone says he will give you $10 to mow his grass, then the $10 is your wage when you actually get the grass cut. Is that a gift? No, you earned it. What's the difference between a gift and a wage? You get a gift for doing nothing. Someone gives you something for a special occasion or just out of the blue.*

Now read Ephesians 4:28 together. *What is a main reason the Bible gives us for working hard and earning wages? What are we supposed to do with the money we earn? We have to pay our bills, but we're also supposed to be generous with helping other people. It's nice to be able to pay your bills, but there's an extra special kind of feeling when you work hard to earn some money and then hand it over to someone who desperately needs it.*

Activity

Beforehand, you'll need to contact people who may have an odd job that they are willing to pay the kids to do. And don't underestimate what kids are capable of. One of the points of this activity is for them to work hard. Assure the people you connect with that there will be adult supervision at all times. Agree on an amount they will pay the kids, but also clearly communicate that the kids will not be keeping the money. They will be giving all of it away to someone or to an organization they decide on before beginning.

IDEAS FOR POSSIBLE PROJECTS:

- cleaning a fence row
- pulling weeds
- spreading mulch
- cleaning out a storage barn

- setting up for a garage sale
- sorting through clothes
- helping pack for a move

Sit down with the kids and explain the project they can do to earn some money. *Do we need any special equipment or supplies?* Get them involved in the planning and then set a time to get together to complete the task.

Read through Ephesians 4:8 again. *We're going to work hard at this project, and we're going to earn $X. Each of us has food to eat, a place to live, and plenty of toys. So what does the Bible tell us we should do with our money? We want to follow Ephesians 4:8 and be generous with the money we earn…just because we can!* Give the kids several choices of what they can do with the money to help someone in need. Let them make the final decision on what it will be used for, and if possible, they should participate in delivering it.

Debrief

Always make sure you sit down with the kids when everything is done so that they can react. This is extremely important!! (I rarely use 2 exclamation points, but that's how important this is.)

- *What was difficult about the work we did?*
- *Did you get tired?*
- *How did you feel when the job was completely done?*
- *Why did you choose to give the money to ________?*
- *What do you think they will do with the money?*
- *How did you feel about working that hard to help someone else?*
- *Do you think you would do it again?*

Labor Day is intended to be a tribute to American workers and the contributions they have made to the strength and prosperity of the United States. In the late 1800s, a time that is known as the Industrial Revolution, most working class people put in 12 hours a day, 7 days a week, and children as young as 5 worked the long hours. Unions were formed at this time to give workers a voice in their pay, working conditions, and hours. Out of that time came Labor Day—a paid day off. Under President Grover Cleveland, it was made a legal holiday by Congress in 1896 and is now the first Monday in September ("Labor Day").

CRUSH FEAR

Scripture:

For God has not given us a spirit of fear and timidity, but of power, love and self-discipline (2 Timothy 1:7, NLT).

Supplies Needed:

- black disposable cups

Activity

This activity seems so simplistic, but kids absolutely love doing it.

The kids will name things that frighten them about Halloween. Before beginning the list, set guidelines that no giggling or ridiculing is allowed. When I casually asked a large group of people of all ages what frightened them, 55% (including adults) were frightened of clowns. So there are all kinds of things that are real fears that others may think are somewhat ridiculous.

On the floor in front of them, the children will each line up 3 black disposable cups, spacing them at least 8" apart. (The black cups remind me of witches' hats, so we're going to smash them to smithereens.) When the leader says, "CRUSH!" the kids will yell out one of the things listed and stomp on a cup. With each cup they crush, they'll yell out another thing associated with Halloween that frightens them. There should be complete mayhem, shouting and crushing as all 3 cups are demolished.

When that round of crushing is done, the kids will list things that cause them fear in everyday life. *What is it that you're afraid of?* (being alone, the dark, not having friends, parents splitting up, getting lost, messing up on a test) Repeat the above black cup crushing activity, only this time they will shout out the everyday fears they have.

Let's Talk

When you crushed the cups, how did that make you feel? Did you feel powerful? Read 2 Timothy 1:7. *Does God want us to be afraid? He offers His Spirit to live inside us, and there is none more powerful than God. So why should we be afraid of anything or any situation when we have the Almighty Powerful God living inside of us? Fear is a tool of Satan. If he can get you to think you do not have the power to face your fear, then he's got you doubting God's power.*

Also help the kids realize that when they cause others to be fearful—at Halloween or any other time—they are being used by Satan. *Satan knows that if he causes you to fear, he is causing you to doubt God's power.*

Place one more black cup in front of the kids. Together they will shout, "Satan, I am not afraid. I have God's power in me!" Then crush that last cup with all your might and give a shout of victory!

DRY BONES

Scriptures:

Then He said to me, "Son of man, these bones are the whole house of Israel; behold, they say, 'Our bones are dried up and our hope has perished. We are completely cut off'" (Ezekiel 37:11, NASB).

"I will put My Spirit within you and you will come to life, and I will place you on your own land. Then you will know that I, the Lord, have spoken and done it," declares the Lord (Ezekiel 37:14, NASB).

Supplies Needed:

- straight (no-bend) drinking straws
- chenille sticks
- scissors

Activity Part 1

For this activity you want straws that do NOT have the accordion segment that enables them to bend. Give each child 5 or 6 straws and instruct them to make a body form by laying the straws out. They will more than likely use one straw for the torso, one for each arm, one for each leg, and then somehow try to configure a head. Do NOT give them access to scissors at this time.

Let's Talk

This figure you have here looks like a skeleton, kind of. Can you move it? Is there any life in it at all? This is an example of how so many people live their lives. They are beaten down by challenging things that have happened to them, and they lose hope that life can ever be any different.

Tell the story of Ezekiel's vision of the dry bones coming to life from Ezekiel 37:1-14. If ever there were a Halloween-ish type story in the Bible, this is it! Skeletons galore! *Although Halloween can be scary and dark, this is a story of how God can take the darkest, most lifeless times in our lives and restore our hope.*

What is hope? Hope is when you have confidence that God is going to keep His promise to be faithful in walking with you. It's looking to the future knowing that no matter what happens, eternity with God is yours, and there's no way it can get better than that!

The Scripture says Ezekiel saw dry bones…really, really dry bones. That's how the Word of God describes somebody who feels completely hopeless. But what did God tell Ezekiel to do to the dry bones? Did He tell him to put them in water? No, watering a dry bone won't do anything. God told Ezekiel to breathe into the bones, and when he did, they came back to life. Even when you feel like you have no hope that the future can be better, you can call on God, and He will breathe hope into you. Like CPR brings air back into a body that is dying, God will revive anyone who calls on Him to bring back their hope. God will breathe His Spirit into you. Nothing is too difficult for God! Absolutely nothing! With Him there is new life and endless possibilities.

Activity Part 2

Now the kids will cut their straws into 1" and 2" pieces. Provide them with chenille sticks that they will thread through the various lengths of straws. The object is for them to create a skeleton, but this skeleton will be able to move. It will have life to it! They can cut their chenille sticks, if necessary, but they should twist them together so the entire body holds together. The chenille sticks will make it possible for the "joints" of the skeleton to bend and move.

- *How is this skeleton different than the one you made at the beginning?*
- *When have you felt hopeless? Or when have you noticed one of your friends feeling hopeless—like life will never get better?* (parents' divorce, someone close to you dies, can't make good grades no matter how hard you try)
- *How does God give you hope? How does He revive your "dry bones"?*

OBSTACLES GALORE

Scripture:

Dear brothers and sisters, when troubles of any kind come your way, consider it an opportunity for great joy. For you know that when your faith is tested, your endurance has a chance to grow. So let it grow, for when your endurance is fully developed, you will be perfect and complete, needing nothing (James 1:2-4, NLT).

Supplies Needed:

- 1-person trampoline
- 4 bales of hay
- 2 large foam dice
- 3 inner tubes
- tables
- black cloth
- poker chips
- 2 baby spoons
- tub of sand
- 6 dowel rods
- 6 pool noodles
- 4 little step-up stools
- several large appliance boxes
- zip-ties or packing tape
- small pumpkins–one for each child
- permanent marker

Activity

Oh my goodness, this is so much fun! Set up a big obstacle course, keeping in mind the age and abilities of the kids who will be participating. The bigger the better! It needs to be big, and it needs to be a little complicated. "Go big or go home!"—Don't do it halfway. Feel free to modify your obstacle course, using what you have available, but the suggestions below will give you an idea of where to start. Beforehand, use a permanent marker to number a pumpkin for each child. For our example, we'll use 1-15.

Here's our obstacle course:

- The child will roll 2 large foam dice to find out how many times he/she is to jump on the trampoline before moving on.
- Jump over a bale of hay.
- Hop through 3 inner tubes laid next to one another.
- Crawl under a table draped with black cloth, from one end to the other.
- The kids will weave in and out of the pool noodles. (Stick 6 dowel rods in the ground, and then slide pool noodles over them so the noodles are standing vertical. They should be about 2' apart. Feel free to use more!)
- Find a poker chip down in a tub of sand by digging with a baby spoon.
- Walk on top of 4 one-step stools without touching the ground in between.
- Set up 3 bales of hay—stacked 2-high with 1 next to it—to create a giant stair. The kids will climb from the 1 bale to the 2-high and then jump off.
- Make a long tube by connecting several cardboard appliance boxes. The kids will crawl through. (You may need to secure the boxes together with duct tape, packing tape, or zip-ties.)
- The kids will run to a group of pumpkins (that have been numbered on the bottom) and choose one to take to the finish line, where they will wait for all the kids to finish the obstacle course.
- *Hey, what else are you going to add to make your obstacle course even bigger?*

Let's Talk

All the kids have a pumpkin with a number on it. They should set those pumpkins out in front of them right now.

Whew! That was some obstacle course! Obstacles can certainly wear you out, can't they? The situations that come up in our lives seem like obstacles that keep us from doing what we want to do, and they can wear us out also! Read James 1:2-4. *What does this passage of Scripture say about obstacles we come across? It says to "bring 'em on!" Yeah! Don't run away from them. Run right at 'em. God promises that if we will depend on Him and follow what His Word says, those obstacles are only going to make us stronger. Going through trials—when we go through them with God—makes our faith stronger. How many of you want to have a stronger faith?*

Let's talk about some obstacles. Create a random drawing system to choose numbers (1-15) of the number of pumpkins/kids you have. Draw out a number and the child with that number on his/her pumpkin will give a response. After that, other kids can contribute their thoughts also. If you have more than 15 kids, then create more situations or break the kids into duplicate groups. After you get the "yes/no" answer, ask: "Why is this an obstacle?" and "How can it make your faith stronger?"

1. You are told you must clean up your room before going outside. Suddenly, you get the idea to shove all the mess in your closet. Will you do that?
2. You are in a carpool with 5 other kids. The first few days you have smelled something funny. You think you smell alcohol on the mother's breath. Do you tell your parents?
3. Some kids are talking about God in a way that is both unkind and untrue. Will you speak up?
4. A friend of yours wants to tell you a secret, but first you must promise not to tell. You promise. Then the friend tells you he is sneaking beer out of the refrigerator. Will you tell anyone?
5. You have heard that a certain hit song uses nasty language. You know your parents would never want you to listen to it. You get the chance to hear the song. Do you listen to it?
6. You get home late from school and eat dinner in your room because you have extra homework. You don't like what your mother has made for dinner, but she says you have to eat it anyway. The dog comes in your room, sniffing and looking hungry. Do you give the dog your dinner?
7. You just failed a very big math test, so it requires your parent's signature. You know if they see it, they will cancel your ski trip this weekend with a good friend's family. Will you forge the signature?
8. Your big brother has been mean to you. He has just finished raking leaves into a big pile. You know he'd have extra work to do if you jumped in the pile, but it would be so much fun. Will you do it?
9. You see someone you like cheating during a test. The person looks up and knows you saw him. Will you tell the teacher?
10. You have a friend at your house. Your mom reminds you that you told her you would unload the dishwasher and set the table. You have not done either. Will you take care of those chores now?
11. You have a very good friend who knows nothing about God. You really want to invite the friend to church, but you're afraid your friend will say "no." Will you invite your friend anyway?
12. You are at an arcade, and you give the manager a dollar. He gives you 5 quarters in return, instead of 4. Do you tell him about the mistake he made?
13. You want a certain brand of tennis shoes. Your mother says she cannot afford them and would like to buy a less expensive pair. Will you argue for the more expensive shoes?

14. You are in class. The person behind you was talking, but you got in trouble for it. The teacher doesn't want to talk about it. Will you keep trying to clear yourself?

15. You are home alone. A friend who lives on the next block calls and asks you to come over and see his brand new puppy. Your parents told you to stay home. Your friend wants you to come just for a few minutes. Will you go?

PUMPKIN GOSPEL

Scriptures:

For this is how God loved the world: He gave his one and only Son, so that everyone who believes in him will not perish but have eternal life. God sent his Son into the world not to judge the world, but to save the world through him (John 3:16-17, NLT).

This means that anyone who belongs to Christ has become a new person. The old life is gone; a new life has begun! (2 Corinthians 5:17, NLT).

Supplies Needed:

- big pumpkin
- plastic tablecloth
- wet rags/wipes/towels
- jigsaw with fine blade
- candle
- matches
- bucket

You'll need a large pumpkin—the larger the better—because you want to have lots of stuff from the inside to work with.

Beforehand, cut the eyes and mouth out of the pumpkin, but put the pieces back in as plugs. You want to make these as clean-cut as possible, so they are barely noticeable.

Display the pumpkin, but put the cut side toward you, so the kids can't see that it's been tampered with. Also, have the top (lid) already cut, but sitting on the pumpkin when you start.

Let's Talk

The pumpkin represents your life. From the outside, you're a pretty good-looking kid. Sometimes you get a little messy from playing outside, but that's not too difficult to clean up. (Wipe the outside of the pumpkin off to remove any dirt.) *Let's see what you look like on the inside, though. The Bible says that all of us have sinned and done things that don't please God. When we sin, it's like we have all kinds of yuck inside us. The inside of this pumpkin is pretty yucky too.*

Kids aren't even aware that some of the things they do displease God. They will take turns pulling out one handful of pumpkin innards. As they do, they should tell one thing that displeases God (a sin). This can be something they themselves are guilty of, or it can be something they have observed others doing. Have a bucket handy for the innards to be thrown into. You should demonstrate the first handful being pulled from the pumpkin, and be glad to get rid of it by smacking it into the bucket. (Have a wet rag ready to wipe off hands.)

We all have things we're guilty of inside us. The only way to get rid of the guilt from doing those things is to ask God to forgive you. When you do something wrong, you should be punished for it, right? And God should punish you for not obeying Him, right? God is total love and can't be with sin. So our punishment would be to be away from God forever. I don't want that, do you? God doesn't want that either, but your sin has to be punished.

God loves us so much that He gave up His Son in heaven and sent Him to live on Earth and die on the cross. But Jesus didn't need to be punished for anything because He had never sinned. Instead, His death was punishment for you and me. If you believe Jesus is God's Son and that He died for your punishment, you ask God to forgive you of all the things you've done that make Him unhappy, and you tell Him that you want to live His way from now on. Then He will take all the yuck in your life and throw it away...just like we did with the pumpkin innards.

What was in that yuck that we threw out? There were seeds, and seeds like to grow, don't they? Your sin is full of seeds—seeds that want to grow in you. They're seeds of anger...fear...hatred... stubbornness...impatience...nasty language... wanting what other people have...all kinds of yucky seeds that you don't want to take root in your life. God gets rid of the yucky seeds too, and the Bible says He makes you a new creation. Read 2 Corinthians 5:17 together.

God isn't finished with you yet. He wants to fill you with His love. It's like a light that He puts inside you. (Place a candle in the pumpkin and light it. Put the lid back on it. Leave it that way long enough for the candlelight to go out. Pull the lid off the pumpkin and let the kids see what happened.)

If you keep the love of God to yourself, it will get weaker and weaker. God wants you to share the love and forgiveness He has given you. You do that by telling other people about what has happened in your life and by watching for opportunities to help others. (Relight the candle. Remove the eyes and mouth plugs and turn the pumpkin around to see the happy face.) *You are a happy person when God forgives your sins and when you share His love with others.*

BELLY CRAWL

Scripture:

There is no greater love than to lay down one's life for one's friends (John 15:13, NLT).

Supplies Needed:

- Six 5-gallon buckets
- 3 long pieces of 2" x 4" boards

Activity

Set up 2 5-gallon buckets about 5 feet apart. Place a 2" x 4" board across them. Set up 2 more buckets with a board across them 20-25 feet away. Do the same for the third set. The boards should just be high enough off the ground that the kids can lay on the ground and "slither like a snake" under the board, much like soldiers do in training.

The kids will take turns running and slithering through this course. They will run to the first set of buckets and board, drop to the ground 3 feet back from the board, and then do the belly crawl under the board. As they are crawling, they have to shout like a soldier: "There is no greater love than to lay down one's life for one's friends!" Once they have completely cleared the board, they will jump up and run to the next board where they will do the same thing, shouting, "There is no greater love than to lay down one's life for one's friends!" Jump up, and finish the course by doing the belly crawl under the third board and repeating the proclamation verse.

Each time a participant gets under one of the raised boards and heads to the next one, a new participant can start the course. You don't have to wait for the person to completely finish before starting the next child.

Let's Talk

Read together John 15:13. *What do you think this verse means? On Veterans Day we can read this verse and think about all the men and women who willingly were part of the military, many just being ready in case they were needed. Some went to war and others didn't, but all of them were willing to lay down their lives for the freedoms we enjoy in this country.*

In this verse, Jesus is teaching His disciples about how much they should love each other. In order to show people we truly mean it when we say we love them, we might have to do something really difficult or something that makes us uncomfortable. Sometimes it means doing something dangerous... like being a missionary in a place where Christians are hated.

What would you be willing to do for a friend who needed your help? Would you give up going to something special if your friend needed you? Would you miss recess to help someone with a subject they were having trouble with? What would you be willing to give up...or lay down...to show your love for someone else?

BUILD A FORTRESS

Scripture:

The Lord is my rock, my fortress and my deliverer; my God is my rock, in whom I take refuge, my shield and the horn of my salvation. He is my stronghold, my refuge and my savior—from violent people you save me. I called to the Lord, who is worthy of praise, and have been saved from my enemies (2 Samuel 22:2-4, NIV).

Supplies Needed:

- really large pieces of cardboard
- wide paint brushes
- paints (shades of gray, black, browns)
- small containers
- drop cloths
- paper wads
- dry sponges

The kids will build their own fortress by painting large pieces of cardboard to look like a stone wall. It's best if someone sketches out the large alternating blocks, so the kids have a guideline to go by. Encourage them to blend the paints—shades of gray, browns, and black—to make it look more like stones. Sponge painting would also work for this. Oh my goodness, kids love doing this!

After the paint dries, some kids can be behind the fortress and others will be across the room, launching paper wads or dry sponges across the wall. And they love this too!

Let's Talk

How did it feel to be protected by the wall when the paper wads and sponges were coming at you? Read 2 Samuel 22:2-4 together. *How do these verses remind you of being behind your cardboard fortress wall?*

Verse 4 says that when David called to the Lord, he was saved from his enemies. Our enemies can be actual soldiers on the other side during a war. That's why we have Veterans Day—to remember all the men and women who served our country in the military and were willing to do whatever was needed of them, whether it was in a battle or taking care of something here in our country. A veteran is someone who took time out of his or her life to serve in the military.

Sometimes, our enemies are not in the uniform of a soldier. What other kinds of enemies do we have? Anything Satan throws at you is an enemy. We're talking about an enemy being anything or anyone who tries to get you to stop following our General—the Almighty God. So what are your enemies right now? When we have an enemy, what does this scripture say we are to do? We get behind our fortress and let God be our protection. We call on Him, and He will help us fight our enemies.

FOLLOW AND SERVE

Scripture:

Anyone who wants to serve me must follow me, because my servants must be where I am. And the Father will honor anyone who serves me (John 12:26, NLT).

Supplies Needed:

- foil casserole pan
- ingredients for main dish
- nonstick spray
- appropriate cooking utensils

Let's Talk

Today we celebrate Veterans Day by honoring those who have served in the military. What did I just say that veterans have done? They served! As a soldier, do you get to do whatever you want, whenever you want? No, you have to follow the orders of the officer in charge. So we celebrate veterans who have "followed" in order to "serve."

Read John 12:26 together. *Jesus is speaking in this verse. How does this verse remind you of veterans? The verse says we should follow Jesus and serve Him, and veterans are honored because they followed and served. Veterans, though, followed and served the military officers who were over them. The Bible tells us to follow and serve Jesus. He's a much higher officer than any in the military!*

We're going to do a project today where you will need to follow me exactly, and together we will be able to serve someone in Jesus' name. The Bible tells us to take care of those who are hungry, sick, and need our help. Identify someone who would benefit from receiving a meal.

Project

Kids love to cook and it's so good for them, especially if it means they are serving others! The kids are going to prepare a main dish that they can take to someone who is sick or to a family that needs help. You can use the recipe described here, or you can use one you are familiar with that is simple to construct. This is best done in small groups of no more than 3 kids per adult. That way, everyone gets to participate—everyone gets to follow and serve.

The adult will demonstrate one step of the recipe, followed by one or two of the kids doing the same thing to the recipe. So keep in mind that the leader will add about one-third of that ingredient, and then give the kids the chance to add the rest of it. Go step-by-step and do not get ahead of yourself. It's fun to refer to the kids throughout the making of the recipe as Private _______ (add their name) and use a military commander voice.

Ingredients:

- 1 lb. ground beef
- 1 24-oz. jar of marinara sauce
- 2 T. basil
- 2 T. parsley flakes
- package of refrigerated ravioli
- 8 oz. mozzarella cheese
- 2 T. Parmesan cheese

STEP 1:
Spray pan with nonstick spray. Boil a large pot of water.

Step 2:
Brown the ground beef and pour off grease.

Step 3:
Add the marinara sauce, basil, and parsley to the meat.

Step 4:
Boil the ravioli for 5 minutes and drain. Put it back in the pot.

Step 5:
Add the meat mixture to the ravioli and lightly stir.

Step 6:
Put half the mixture in the baking pan. Layer ¾ c. of mozzarella on top.

Step 7:
Add the other half of the mixture and top with the rest of the mozzarella, along with the Parmesan cheese.

If you want to deliver this hot to someone, bake it for 25 minutes at 350°.

If at all possible, take the kids with you to deliver the dish. As kids learn about serving, it's important for them to experience actually handing the dish to the person who needs it.

What did you learn as you put the recipe together? How did it make you feel to serve in this way? How do you think the person receiving this meal will feel? Would you ever want to do this again?

SHOES OF PEACE

Scripture:

Put on the full armor of God, so that you can take your stand against the devil's schemes…and with your feet fitted with the readiness that comes from the gospel of peace (Ephesians 6:11 & 15, NIV).

Supplies Needed:

- large assortment of different kinds of shoes
- music

Let's Talk

On Veterans Day, we honor all the people who have been in the military and who have been willing to fight for the freedom of our country. Why is it that soldiers go to battle? They want peace. They want life to be safe and free. They want to be part of bringing peace to a situation where two sides are against one another.

In the Civil War, the worst problem the soldiers had with their uniforms was their shoes. The shoes wore out from marching so much, going in and out of water, and they didn't have a way to replace them. Eventually, many of the men marched barefoot, leaving bloody marks behind them from their tortured feet. Soldiers who were killed on the battlefield would often have their shoes taken by other soldiers. In the South, occasionally the men who did not have shoes would be put together to march in the grass instead of on the roads.

The Bible tells us to wear a different kind of shoe when we fight. Read Ephesians 6:11 and 15. *There are several pieces to our spiritual armor, but one of them is the Shoes of the Gospel of Peace. Why do we wear shoes? To protect our feet from splinters, rocks, puddles, and hot asphalt. Jesus is the way to peace with God. God cannot tolerate sin, and we have all sinned. Jesus took the punishment for our sin, so we can come back to a relationship with God. The sin is gone. The sin is what caused conflict with God. Jesus got rid of that conflict and brought peace. That's the "Gospel" or the "Good News" of peace.*

You don't just sit around with your shoes on. No, you move around when you have your shoes on. So why would shoes be used in the armor of God as the Gospel of Peace? We need to go and share the Gospel with others, so they can have God's peace also. It doesn't matter how old you are or what job you have, you can wear your spiritual armor of the Gospel of peace and share the peace that Jesus offers with others.

Game

Gather as many different kinds of shoes as you can. The bigger the variety, the more fun this is. Play a game much like Hot Potato. Each round, though, you will put a different shoe in the game to be passed. When the music stops, the person with the shoe will share a way that someone wearing this shoe might be able to bring peace to a situation. (Example: tennis shoe—refuse to fight over a call the referee made in a basketball game) Always open it up for anyone else to add their comments or ideas.

If you're playing with preschoolers, they can identify what kind of shoe it is and say, "Jesus brings peace." This is a great place to start with little ones.

At the 11th hour of the 11th day of the 11th month (November) in 1918, World War I came to an end as the Allied nations and Germany signed an agreement. A special day to honor all those who had served in that war was designated. It was called Armistice Day and fell on November 11 each year. In 1926 the US Congress declared it an official federal holiday. After the US involvement in World War II and the Korean War, the name was changed to Veterans Day to honor all those—living or deceased—who had served in the military. On this day we honor everyone who has served in one of the armed forces.

("The Origins of Veterans Day")

CORNUCOPIAS

Scripture:

O Lord my God, you have performed many wonders for us. Your plans for us are too numerous to list. You have no equal. If I tried to recite all your wonderful deeds, I would never come to the end of them (Psalm 40:5, NLT).

Supplies Needed:

- cornucopia basket horn
- one each of a variety of vegetables and fruits

The cornucopia is a basket horn that holds a collection of fruits and vegetables from the harvest. People have always been thankful for a good harvest, and the filled cornucopia is a reminder of how God provided.

Activity

The kids can work by themselves or with a partner or two to complete this exercise. Place an empty cornucopia on a table where it will be displayed when completed. Then spread out a big variety of fruits and vegetables on a separate table.

Each time we learn something about God—who He is, how He works, how He changes people—we can be very thankful. He is drawing us closer to Himself as we chase after Him. But, just like all things that we learn, sometimes we don't realize what has happened, and we don't take the time to be thankful for it.

The kids will use the fruits and vegetables as object lessons to describe something they have learned about God. In an object lesson, you think about the characteristics of the object and then relate one of those characteristics to the point you are trying to make. In this instance, the kids will think of the characteristics of a piece of fruit or a vegetable and then relate one to something they are thankful that they learned about God.

Some examples:

- Bunch of grapes – Each grape represents someone in our church. We are thankful we can come together, and be a bunch, to tell others about Jesus.
- Orange – You can divide the orange into segments. We can thank God the fruit of the Spirit is like those segments—all part of the whole—love, joy, peace, patience, kindness, goodness, gentleness, faithfulness, and self-control.
- Green beans – You pick them and a few days later they are ready to pick again. The green bean plants keep producing more and more beans! Thank You, God, that people keep coming to know You. We should never be satisfied when one person becomes a believer because there are always more people who need to hear the Good News.

The child or small group will choose a fruit/vegetable and come up with their thankfulness statement. They will share it with the other kids/groups and then place that piece in the cornucopia.

When you are finished, the cornucopia will be full, and it will remind you to thank God for all you have learned about Him! That truly is a reason to be thankful this Thanksgiving.

COVERED WITH THANKSGIVING

Scripture:

The Lord is my strength and shield. I trust him with all my heart. He helps me, and my heart is filled with joy. I burst out in songs of thanksgiving (Psalm 28:7, NLT).

Supplies Needed:

- paper
- pencils

Let's Talk

Sometimes when you have a problem, you can't get your mind off of it. The longer you think about it, the bigger it feels. You start thinking about all the "what ifs"....What if this never gets better? What if they never speak to me again? What if I can't learn how to do math? Some people let their problem take over their thoughts and attitudes, and that sucks the joy right out of their life.

The kids will write a problem on a piece of paper and describe it completely. Lay it on the floor. Read Psalm 28:7.

- *Who is God to you? Is He the One who gives you strength? Do you trust Him with all your heart?*
- *If you rely on God for your strength and protection, and if you trust Him, what will He do? He will help you! He will give you joy!*
- *When you realize that God is helping you, what is your response? Do you burst out with thankfulness? Do you cover Him with your gratitude?*

The verse is a promise. If you trust God, He will help you. Plain and simple. Thanksgiving is a day when we should especially think about being thankful. There is nothing we should be more thankful for than the way our God loves us and takes care of us.

So let's just cover that problem that's on the floor with our gratitude. Write on individual pieces of paper what you are thankful for. When you complete each piece of thankfulness paper, lay it on top of the problem paper on the floor. Keep writing and placing additional thankfulness papers on top of the problem paper. "Thank You, God, that You are always with me." "Thank You, God, that I have wonderful friends who believe in You too." "Thank You, God, that You make me strong when I don't think I can get through something." "Thank You, God, for stopping me from saying mean things when I'm angry."

All of these gratitude papers have covered up the problem paper, and you can hardly see it now...maybe not at all. When we concentrate on being thankful, we don't concentrate so much on the problem we're facing. So, when you start focusing on a problem, back up and thank God out loud for who He is and how He has helped you. Let Him fill you with joy instead of worry.

MARSHMALLOW MADNESS

Scripture:

Be thankful in all circumstances, for this is God's will for you who belong to Christ Jesus
(1 Thessalonians 5:18, NLT).

Supplies Needed:

- regular size marshmallows
- glass of water
- microwave
- paper plate

In every situation we have the opportunity to react with an attitude of: I deserve this, what's the big deal, anger, frustration, or in a whole bunch of other negative ways. Or, and this is a great big OR, you can react with gratitude…no matter what the situation is—happy or not-so-happy. You get to choose how you will respond.

Activity

Place one regular-sized marshmallow in a glass of water. It will float because it is filled with air. Remove the marshmallow. Now give the children their own marshmallow. Ask them to name negative ways they could react to something that happens in their life. Each time someone shares a way he/she could react—a way other than being thankful—the kids will give their marshmallow one big squish. Each one of these negative squishes will make the marshmallow smaller and smaller. Eventually, the marshmallows will become small little balls. Drop one of these in the glass of water. What does it do? It sinks!

Read 1 Thessalonians 5:18. *When does this verse tell us to be thankful? What does it mean by "all" circumstances?* (This would be a great time to tell Corrie ten Boom's story of the fleas in the barracks at the concentration camp. See page 69.) *When we live with thankful hearts, no matter if the situation brings happiness at the moment or not, something very different happens to us. We don't have that sinking feeling. Let's look at a different marshmallow to show us.*

Place a fresh marshmallow on a paper plate and put it in a microwave. The kids should gather round to watch through the window. Turn the microwave on and watch what happens to the marshmallow. As it gets warmer and warmer, it gets bigger and fluffier. *Which marshmallow do you like the most—the one that sank in the glass or this one that grew in the microwave?*

God will give you the strength to be thankful in ALL circumstances, but the desire has to come from within you. As we live out gratitude to God in all circumstances, we will grow closer to Him because it takes trust and faith to say, "God, I don't understand this, but I am going to be thankful that You are sharing this time with me."

TO BEND OR NOT TO BEND

Scripture:

If you love me, you will keep my commandments (John 14:15, ESV).

Supplies Needed:

- 2 turkey leg bones
- vinegar
- tall jar with a lid

Instructions:

Those 2 big turkey legs look so yummy on the Thanksgiving table… and they are. Go ahead; eat every little morsel off those bones. Then, when you've eaten your fill and pulled the rest off for later, clean the 2 leg bones. Pull off anything that isn't the turkey bone. Run them under warm water until you've got two nice shiny turkey bones.

You'll need a jar that's large enough to hold one entire bone and still be able to screw on the cap. Once the bone is in the jar, fill the jar with vinegar, completely submerging the leg. Now put the lid on tightly, because you don't want to be getting whiffs of vinegar every time you pass this jar.

So what do you do with the other leg bone? Put it in a ziplock bag and toss it in the freezer. We'll get it back out in several weeks.

Leave the turkey bone in the jar of vinegar for 3-4 weeks. That's when you can pull it out and rinse it off.

Retrieve the other turkey bone from the freezer and thaw it out.

Try to bend each of the turkey legs. The one that has been soaking in vinegar for 4 weeks will be rubbery. Weird! The other bone will not want to bend at all.

Let's Talk

There are some things in life that we can "bend" on, and then there are other things that we absolutely can't bend on. How do we decide whether it's okay to be like the rubbery turkey leg or we've got to be like the hard turkey leg? When it's okay to bend on something, we call that compromise. Compromise is when you're willing to change and agree with someone else's ideas.

When the Pilgrims and the Wampanoag Indians came together for the first Thanksgiving meal, it was probably a political kind of meeting more than a party. They were trying to figure out how to get along in the same land. One of the things they had to do was to compromise on who would be allowed on what land, what was okay for each one to do, and how they would live close to one another without causing problems. Compromise was a big part of the first Thanksgiving.

Read John 14:15. *This verse helps us figure out when we can compromise. It says that we are to keep God's commandments. We can compromise—we can bend—when the compromise doesn't disappoint God and go against His commandments.* (Bend the turkey leg to demonstrate compromise.) *So, when you want to go to McDonald's and your sister wants to go to Wendy's, is it okay to compromise and go to Wendy's?* (Bend the turkey leg again.)

Sure, because you are not disobeying any of God's commandments. Name some other times when it's okay to compromise—or bend.

But we cannot compromise if it causes us or others to sin. If the compromise hurts you or someone else, you can't choose to compromise. You cannot bend. (Hold up the hard turkey leg and act like you're going to try to bend it.) *When a friend tells you that you can take the tickets hanging out of the machine at Chuck E. Cheese, even though they aren't yours, can you compromise and say it's okay to take them?* (Show the hard turkey leg again.) *No, because that would be stealing, and that's against God's commandments. Name some other situations when you should not compromise or bend.*

It is a good thing to learn to compromise so that we get along with people better, but there's a line we cannot cross. We cannot go against God's commandments just to keep our friends happy with us. When we check God's commandments, we can know when to compromise, when to bend (bend the turkey bone), *and when we cannot compromise or bend* (hold up the hard turkey bone).

At Thanksgiving time, we can be thankful for God's commandments that give us the guidelines for when we can bend and when we can't.

THANKFUL FOR FLEAS

Corrie ten Boom shared a story in her book *The Hiding Place* that reminds us all to take 1 Thessalonians 5:18 to heart, where the Scripture instructs us to be thankful in all circumstances.

Corrie tells of being in the barracks of the concentration camp along with her sister, Betsie, when they started being bit by what turned out to be fleas…lots and lots of fleas. They seemed intolerable.

Betsie prayed that God would show them how to tolerate the fleas. In responding to that prayer, God brought a verse, 1 Thessalonians 5:18, to mind. It was a verse they had read together that morning. The verse had not only said to be thankful in all circumstances, but to rejoice in the midst of them.

Betsie insisted that they begin thanking God for everything about this horrible place where they were now living. Corrie hesitantly followed her sister's lead. Instead of thanking God for the women in the barracks, they thanked God for how crowded it was because they would be able to share about the Lord with more people.

And then Betsie did what Corrie felt was unimaginable. She thanked God for those pesky fleas. Corrie admittedly thought Betsie had gone too far with that one.

Meanwhile, the sisters started a worship service in their barracks—something they could receive horrible punishment for if they were discovered. More and more women joined in. The surveillance on the barracks on both sides of theirs was constant, but for some strange reason, this barracks was hardly ever interrupted or checked on. Why was that?

One night, Betsie seemed very pleased and Corrie questioned her unusual excitement. Betsie's smile came from finding out why the guards had not been eager to check on their particular barracks. Her discovery came when they had asked a supervisor to come in and answer some questions they had about the work they were assigned to do. Neither the guards nor the supervisor would come in. Why?

Because the barracks was infested with fleas! Those fleas that seemed to have no purpose except to torment them were actually an umbrella of grace that God provided so the women of that barracks could worship Him.

Thanksgiving Trivia

President Abraham Lincoln declared Thanksgiving a national holiday in 1863.

According to Edward Winslow, who wrote a first-hand account of the "First" Thanksgiving, when the Pilgrims had dinner with the Wampanoag Indians, they gathered "wild fowl" prior to the dinner. We don't know if that was turkey or some other bird.

Journals indicate that there were about 90 men at the "First" Thanksgiving dinner—which lasted 3 days! There were probably no women at the dinner, as this was more of a political meeting between the Pilgrims and the Indians than a fun-filled get-together.

CHRISTMAS STORY BOXES

Instructions

The kids will be very excited to hear the Christmas story told in this manner. Prior to the kids' arrival, you will need to wrap 8 boxes in festive Christmas wrap, but make sure the boxes have lift-off lids. Below are the descriptions of what item goes in each box. Because the gifts need to be opened in order, write a number on the bottom of the box to indicate its position in the sequence. Place the gifts under a Christmas tree (if you have one in your area) and choose one child at a time to find the gift with the next number on it. Each time a child unwraps a gift, they will show everyone what is inside. The leader will then tell about the item and what meaning it has to the story before choosing another child to find the next numbered box. When the story is finished, have the children place the lids back on the boxes and set them under the tree to use again next year.

Box #1: WATCH

"At that time" is how the story of the birth of Jesus begins in the Bible. It was a special time in history. A census was being taken throughout all of the Roman Empire. The Roman Empire covered a huge part of the world, and the emperor wanted to know how many people were in his kingdom.

Box #2: PIECE OF BREAD

This bread reminds us that Bethlehem means the "house of bread." Joseph and Mary had to go to the town that Joseph's family came from, and that town happened to be "the house of bread"—Bethlehem. About 2,700 years before Jesus was born, a prophet named Micah (see Micah 5:2) *told about a ruler who would come from the little village of Bethlehem. God had planned long ago for Jesus to come as our Savior. He even planned the details of how it would happen—that Jesus would be born in Bethlehem. It's interesting that one of the names for Jesus in the Bible is Bread of Life.*

Box #3: BABY DOLL

When Mary and Joseph arrived in Bethlehem, the town was really crowded because many people had traveled there for the same reason Mary and Joseph had. They were part of the census. It was time for Mary to have her baby, but there wasn't a good place for them to stay. It would've been nice to have a quiet, private place, but everything was so noisy and crowded! The only place they could find was a stable, and that's where the baby Jesus was born.

Box #4: SOFT CLOTH

When the baby was born, Mary swaddled Him in soft cloths. Swaddle means to wrap a baby very tightly. That sounds like it would hurt the baby, but actually it's very comforting. A baby who is crying will stop when he or she is swaddled in the right way. Then, instead of putting the baby Jesus in a crib, they laid Him in the feeding trough for the animals. The feeding trough is called a manger.

Box #5: cotton balls, photo of a sheep, or a stuffed sheep

Because Bethlehem was so crowded, the shepherds took their sheep way out on the hills. The noise from the crowds of people in the town would frighten the sheep. Out there, away from everything, the shepherds watched over their sheep and cared for them. The sun went down and the sky was dark. They may have been talking around a campfire and looking at the stars.

Box #6: a piece of gold chenille stick made into a circle

In the middle of the silence and darkness out on the hills, all of a sudden an angel surprised the shepherds. I bet they didn't know whether to run or hide or just freeze in their places. They had never seen an angel! What was going on? The angel told them that they shouldn't be afraid because he had great news. He also told them that they should go into town because a very special baby had just been born. That baby would be the Savior the Scriptures told them about—the Savior they had been waiting for. The angel gave them some clues. He said they would find the baby wrapped in cloths and lying in a manger. (There probably weren't too many babies lying in animal feeding troughs.) Then a whole bunch more angels showed up, and they all started singing praises to God. The sky was full of angels! Unbelievable! They said, "Glory to God in all the heavens, and on earth, peace, good will to men" (from Luke 2:14).

Box #7: straw

The shepherds left their sheep and went to Bethlehem to find the baby that the angel had told them about. Just like the angel said, they found the baby Jesus in a manger, lying on a mattress of straw.

Box #8: heart-shaped ornament

Here's part of the story that we sometimes forget, but it's one of my favorite parts. The Bible tells us that Mary remembered everything she had experienced—every sound, every word, everything she saw, even everything she smelled. Every part of this evening was special. What happened to her that evening would be incredibly important to people forever. She wanted to remember all of it! The Bible says she treasured all of it. She treasured the memory of her baby's little fingers. She treasured the smile on Joseph's face when he held Jesus for the first time. She treasured the sight of the shepherds, sitting in the straw in front of the manger and not wanting to leave. She treasured watching Baby Jesus sleep His very first night on this Earth. She'd never forget this night.

CRYSTAL BORAX ORNAMENT

This is an absolutely beautiful ornament…a little on the heavy side…but really pretty. The main thing you need is 24 hours of patient wait time when the ornament can be totally undisturbed.

Supplies Needed:

- white chenille stick
- dental floss
- new pencil or a piece of dowel rod
- large mouth jar
- tape
- Borax
- boiling water
- food coloring
- thin ribbon

Note: Borax is found in the detergent aisle of your grocery store. It is very important that your jar have a wide mouth and is also deep enough for the shape formed by the chenille stick to be completely submerged.

Instructions:

- Twist a chenille stick into a shape, like a bell or star. Twist the ends together securely, and then push them down flat so no ends are sticking out.
- Test the shape to make sure it will fit through the mouth of the jar without mashing it or changing the shape. If it doesn't fit, you either need a jar with a wider mouth, or you need to make your shape a little smaller.
- Tie one end of a piece of dental floss to the chenille stick shape. Tie the other end to a pencil or dowel rod. Before going any further, set the dowel rod across the mouth of the jar and see how far the shape hangs in the jar. You don't want the chenille stick shape to touch the bottom, but you also want it to be able to be covered with the mixture we'll make in the next step. You can adjust the length of the dental floss by rolling it around the dowel rod. Once you get it adjusted, place a piece of tape across the dental floss to hold it in place. Now take everything out of the jar and set it aside.
- Almost fill the jar with boiling water, but measure it as you go. Add 4 tablespoons of Borax for each cup of water in the jar and then stir…stir… stir. If all the Borax is dissolving, then you need to add some more. You know you have enough Borax when it will no longer dissolve in the boiling water.
- If you leave the water like this, you will have a clear crystal ornament. Stir in some food coloring to make a colored ornament.
- Now lower the chenille shape into the jar and rest the dowel rod across the top of the jar. Make sure your chenille shape is completely submerged.
- Set the jar in a place where it will not be bumped. The crystallization starts within the first hour, and if moved after that, even slightly, the process will be interrupted and will change what your ornament was supposed to look like.
- Let it set there for 18-24 hours. You can watch during that time, BUT DON'T TOUCH!
- Gently lift the dowel rod and pull the chenille shape out of the water. It's quite a bit heavier now, isn't it?
- Clip the dental floss from the ornament and add a loop of ribbon to use as a hanger.

Let's Talk

Whatever gift you give to God this Christmas seems small in comparison to all the incredible things He has created and all the miracles He has done. But God will take what we willingly offer Him, no matter how simple, and will make something absolutely beautiful out of it.

You may think your life isn't much to give the Creator of the Universe. After all, you're just a kid. The chenille stick was a cheap little piece of fuzzy wire when we first started with it. When we handed it over to the jar and the solution and stepped back to wait to see what would happen, it became something awesome that makes us smile. That's exactly what God wants us to do—hand ourselves over to Him, willingly put our lives in His hands, and step back to see what He can do—how He can change us and use us for His glory. Your life will be something awesome that makes God smile if you do that.

GIFT-WRAP GOLF

Supplies Needed:

- unopened rolls of gift wrap
- round plastic ornaments (from the dollar store)
- large red plastic cups
- masking tape

Game

Beforehand, cut the bottom out of 6 large red plastic cups. Put down a piece of masking tape 12-15 feet away from a wall.

Choose 6 players for the game. About a foot away from the wall, place the red plastic cups on their side, with the open bottom facing the wall. The players will each get an unopened roll of gift wrap and the same number of plastic ornaments. When the game begins, the players will be positioned behind the masking tape line. At the signal, they will lay down an ornament on the masking tape line and tee off to putt the ornament into their red cup (not someone else's). They will keep tapping this ornament until they get it to either stay in their cup or pass through it. Dragging the ornament along with the roll of gift wrap is NOT allowed. When one player successfully gets an ornament in his/her cup, the player will yell, "Merry Christmas!" and all play stops. That player will receive 10 points and get the opportunity to receive an additional 10 points by answering one of the following questions.

Note: The ornaments will not roll as expected because of the piece that sticks up where the hanger attaches. That's what makes it unpredictable and fun.

- *What is a census?* (where people are counted)
- *What is a stable?* (a place where animals are kept, a barn)
- *What is a manger?* (a trough that animals eat out of)
- *How many gifts did the wise men give Baby Jesus?* (3)
- *How did the shepherds feel when they saw the angel?* (afraid)
- *What were all the angels doing?* (praising God)
- *Why did Mary and Joseph have to go to Bethlehem?* (to be counted as part of the census because that's where Joseph's family was from)
- *What did the shepherds do when they saw the baby Jesus?* (bowed down to worship Him)
- *What was used for a bed for Baby Jesus?* (manger with straw)
- *What did Mary wrap the baby Jesus in?* (cloths)
- *How did the wise men know where to go?* (followed a star)
- *Name one of the gifts the wise men brought.* (gold, frankincense, myrrh)
- *Name one of the gifts the wise men brought.*
- *Name one of the gifts the wise men brought.*

HOVERING BOTTLE

Scripture:

After they had heard the king, they went on their way, and the star they had seen when it rose went ahead of them until it stopped over the place where the child was (Matthew 2:9, NIV).

Supplies Needed:

- 2-liter bottle (full)
- bottle balancer (available from teachersource.com for about $10)
- clean, flat, level surface
- yellow construction paper star
- tape
- index card
- marker

Experiment

- Set the angled end of the balance board against the table. Your table MUST be level and smooth.
- Insert the neck of a 2-liter bottle through the hole in the board.
- Check to make sure the angled end of the board is resting against the table completely.
- You will be able to feel when the 2-liter bottle is balanced. Gently release it and the bottle will be suspended in midair. If it doesn't seem to want to balance, then your surface is not completely flat. The lightweight plastic tables frequently pose a problem because their surface is a little wavy or bumpy. If the bottle wants to tilt one direction, then raise that end of the surface a little by adding some folded paper under a leg(s) of the table.

Let's Talk

- *Describe what the bottle is doing. Why is this so amazing? Bottles aren't supposed to hang in the air like this, are they?*
- Read Matthew 2:9. *How does this verse remind you of the hovering bottle?*

Tape a construction paper star on the end of the bottle. Point to the table under the star. *What did the wise men find here?* Prior to the activity, write "JESUS" on a folded index card. Set the index card, tent-style, on the table under the star.

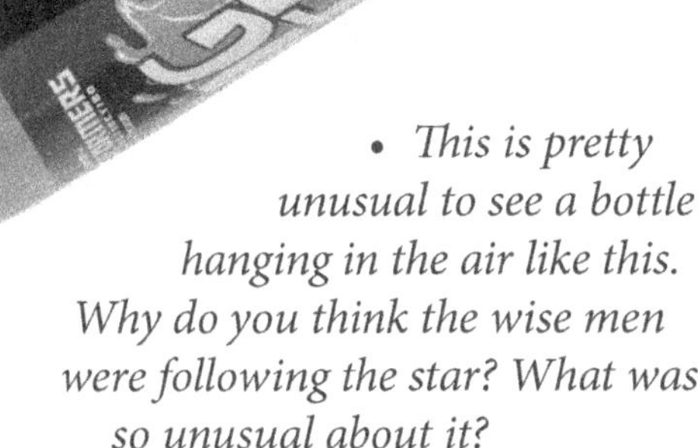

- *This is pretty unusual to see a bottle hanging in the air like this. Why do you think the wise men were following the star? What was so unusual about it?*
- *Why do you think God used a star to "hover" over where the young Jesus was?*

Most of the time, our nativity sets show that the wise men came to the manger, but they actually came later than that. Mary and Joseph and the little Jesus were living in a house by the time the wise men arrived. That's why we didn't put a manger on the table under the star but the card that said "JESUS." How do we know that from reading the Scriptures? Check out verse 11.

Do you think anyone else besides the wise men realized the star was hovering over the house where Jesus was?

WHAT'S MISSING?

Supplies Needed:

- a complete nativity set
- large cookie sheet
- towel

Activity

Lay all the pieces of the nativity set out on the cookie sheet and cover it with a towel.

Gather the children around the covered cookie sheet. Remove the towel and let them look at the pieces for 20 seconds. Now cover it again. The kids will turn their backs to the tray, and the leader will remove one piece and place it where the kids can't see it. Uncover the cookie sheet once again. The kids will try to figure out which piece of the nativity is now missing. The child who identifies the missing piece will then tell what part that piece played in the story of Jesus being born.

On the last round, remove the baby Jesus. When the kids discover that it is the baby Jesus nativity piece that is not on the cookie sheet, then stop to talk.

- *The baby Jesus was missing in our game! Is the baby Jesus ever missing from our Christmas celebrations?*
- *When we looked at all the pieces on the cookie sheet, it wasn't quickly obvious that it was the baby Jesus that wasn't there. We saw all the other pieces. What do we concentrate on at Christmas that keeps us from noticing that Jesus isn't the reason for our celebration?*
- *How can you make sure that Jesus isn't missing from your Christmas?*

SHEPHERD HEADPIECE

Supplies:

- 8-10" piece of ½" elastic
- staple gun
- square yard of lightweight cloth

Instructions:

Shepherd's headpieces are always falling off! Duct tape doesn't work. Neither do staples, hot glue, or safety pins. The answer is very simple! All you need is one square yard of lightweight material (plain or patterned), an 8-10" piece of ½" elastic, and very minimal sewing skills.

Your piece of material does not have to be exact. Anything 3'-4' works well. Put a shirttail hem on all the edges of the piece of material to keep it from raveling (unless 2 of the sides are selvage). At the edge of one side of your fabric, center your piece of elastic. Loosely lay the elastic against the material. Double-stitch the ends of the elastic to the material. You are done!

This is how you put the headpiece on. The kids can easily do this themselves. 1…2…3!

1. Bend over.

2. Place the edge of the material (the edge that has the elastic on it) against your forehead and pull the elastic over your head so that it goes across the back of your head. The material is now hanging down in front of your face.

3. Now stand up quickly, flipping the material that was hanging in front of your face over your head. It will come down your back and should fall in place as the perfect headpiece (with maybe a little "fluffing" on the sides).

THE M&M STORY

Scripture:

Luke 2:1-20

Supplies:

- individual packs of M&Ms or a large bag
- paper plates

Instructions:

Give each child a package of M&Ms or a scoop from a large bag. They will use these candies to engage in the story of Jesus' birth. The kids should open their packs of M&Ms prior to the beginning of the story and pour them on a paper plate. Assure them that there will be a time for eating the candies but not right now.

The Story

The Roman Emperor had spoken. He declared that there would be a tax where people had to go to their hometown. Who had to go to his hometown? "E"very man had to go.

- *Pull out an M&M and turn it so the "M" is sideways to look like an "E". The rough roads were filled with people traveling. What does this "E" stand for? Every man who had to go to his hometown.*

Now hold one M&M so that you can read the "M" because it stands for Mary. Mary was pregnant with a little boy. What color do we think of with baby boys? Blue!

- *Pull out a blue M&M for the baby boy. Mary was pregnant with the baby Jesus in her belly. What does the "M" stand for? Mary. What does the blue M&M stand for? The baby boy, Jesus.*

The journey from Nazareth to their hometown of Bethlehem was no joy ride! On the best of days, the journey was difficult for anyone to make. The roads were dusty, rocky, and uneven. There were scorpions, wild animals, and bandits to watch out for.

- *Pull out a brown M&M. This M&M stands for the dusty roads Mary and Joseph traveled to Bethlehem. There were no rest areas or fast food restaurants where they could take a break. Maybe Mary sat on a donkey, and Joseph led the donkey as he walked. What does the brown M&M stand for? The dusty roads they traveled.*

At least, when they got to Bethlehem, they would be able to relax in a comfortable room…NOT! The town was bursting at the seams with taxpayers! There were people "E"verywhere.

- *Turn ALL your M&Ms sideways to make "E"s for all the people who were everywhere. There was not one room left anywhere in town! The only place Joseph and Mary could find to stay was in the stable of an inn. This is where the animals were kept! This was no fit place for the King of Kings, the Lord of Lords, God's only Son to be born! Why did we turn all the M&Ms so they all looked like "E"s? People were "E"verywhere!*

But there was no choice. Mary was very close to giving birth, and they couldn't let that happen on the street! In fact, Jesus was born that very night! Mary wrapped the baby in soft strips of cloth and placed Him in a manger. She probably kissed the baby's forehead.

- *Pull out all the red M&Ms to remind us of the love Mary had for Baby Jesus. What do the red M&Ms remind you of? Mary's love for her baby.*

- *Pull aside one M&M so that it shows the "M". This "M" stands for "manger." Do you know what a manger is? Is it like a soft, cushy, baby bassinette? Not even close. A manger is a feeding trough that animals eat out of. It was usually filled with hay or straw! What does this "M" stand for? Manger.*

Shepherds were out on the hills around Bethlehem with their sheep. They were out there to find green grass for the sheep to eat.

- *Pull out a green M&M to remind you of the sheep being on the hillsides around Bethlehem. What color M&M reminds you of the sheep? Green, for the grass they ate.*

The night Jesus was born, a group of shepherds were watching their sheep in a field just outside of Bethlehem. It was a peaceful night. Then suddenly a bright light surrounded them. I always think of the light being a bright yellow.

- *Pull out all the yellow M&Ms to remind you of the light the shepherds saw. An angel of the Lord appeared. The shepherds shook in fear! They had never seen anything like this before! The angel comforted them saying, "Fear not, I bring you good news that will bring GREAT JOY to all people! In Bethlehem the Savior of the world has been born! He is Christ the Lord!" (See Luke 2:10-11) The angel told the shepherds that they would find the baby wrapped in cloths and lying in the manger. The disciples were in shock! This was great news! They were filled with joy! What do all these yellow M&Ms remind you of? The bright light from the angel.*

Then the angel who spoke to the shepherds was joined by a whole army of angels!

- *Turn all your M&Ms sideways so that they look like "3"s. If we added all these "3"s together, would that be the number of angels that appeared to the shepherds? No! There were lots more than that! The angels began to praise God, saying, "Glory to God in the highest, and on earth peace, good will to men!" (See Luke 2:14) Why did we turn our M&Ms sideways to make "3"s? There were lots and lots of angels.*

The angels disappeared as quickly as they had come. The shepherds were excited; they couldn't stand still! The peaceful night with the sheep had been turned upside down!

- *Turn all your M&Ms over so they are upside down. This was supposed to be a peaceful quiet night and it was totally opposite, totally upside down, from what it usually was. The shepherds said to each other, "Let's go to Bethlehem right now and see what God has told us about!" (See Luke 2:15) Why did we turn our M&Ms over so they were upside down? This news of Jesus' birth turned the world upside down.*

The shepherds had never left their sheep before, but this was more important! God sent angels to share the good news of the Savior's birth with them! If God took the time to do that, He certainly could protect their sheep! The shepherds hurried to Bethlehem and found Jesus wrapped in cloths, lying in a manger...exactly as the angels had described. The shepherds knelt down to worship the baby Jesus.

- *Turn one of your M&Ms so that it makes a "W". This "W" stands for "worship." What does the "W" stand for? Worship.*

The shepherds were so filled with joy and amazement that they told everyone about what had just happened! Mary heard their story and kept it within herself as she thought about it.

- *Pull aside one of your M&Ms and turn it so you can read the "M" for Mary. Mary kept everything she had seen, heard, and experienced all to herself and enjoyed having those wonderful memories.*

The shepherds ran back to their sheep. The whole way they were leaping, dancing, and praising God for all that had just happened to them. God had cared enough about them to send an army of angels to tell them about Baby Jesus! They had seen the Christ Child—the Savior of the World—with their very own eyes! What color are your eyes?

- *Pull out the M&M that is the color of your eyes (blue, green, brown). They knew the angel's message was real because they had seen Jesus with their own eyes.*

Joy had truly come to the world!

- *Pull out all the orange M&Ms. Now, "orange" you glad we did this!*

SURPRISE STABLE

Supplies Needed:

- gift wrap
- small room
- manger
- swaddled doll
- other materials to create live nativity scene
- 2 actors—Mary and Joseph
- shepherd(s) and lamb—optional

Instructions:

Looking into a manger scene, reading a book, or driving by a live nativity are all nice ways to expose children to the story of God becoming man. But what if you placed the child unexpectedly right in the middle of the scene—using all their senses to experience what it may have been like?

The extravagance of this experience depends totally on how much time, energy, and resources you have to put into it…and also on the talents of people who are willing to help. Designate a room that you will totally clear out and convert into the stable. (The kids should not be able to see inside this room at all.) To disguise what's in the room, wrap the door in wrapping paper with a big bow. This will probably make the kids think there are presents inside or a Christmas tree…or maybe even Santa. They won't be expecting what's behind the door! And the surprise is a big part of the experience.

Think about how the kids—using all 5 senses—could experience Mary and Joseph in awe of the baby Jesus. When the kids come through the wrapped door, close it behind them, and let them be carried away as a participant in that holy night. Here are some things to consider—some creative springboards—to get your thoughts flowing about what to include in the room:

- Paint backgrounds on foam core board or painters' tarps to cover the walls. It is important that the walls be covered to make this feel like an entirely different time and place.
- Mary and Joseph in full costume. They should be talking about all that's happened, occasionally moving around to care for the baby.
- Instead of the traditional looking manger, think about how you could depict one that is more realistic for the time. The manger probably would've been hewn out of stone. You can do this with paper mache or stacking some landscaping blocks.
- Scatter hay over the entire floor. This will provide a distinct smell, as well as a different surface for the kids to walk on.
- Could someone dress as a shepherd and hold a lamb? Don't set the lamb loose, or the kids will be distracted from the baby Jesus. More than likely, the lamb will let out his sweet baby sound. Several shepherds could be sitting around the manger or kneeling to peer in. Make sure you leave room for the kids to join them.
- Taste. Now, this sense may be a little more difficult. What if one of the shepherds offered Mary and Joseph a small loaf of bread from their satchel? Then turn and offer a small piece to each child. Jesus would one day be known as the Bread of Life, and Bethlehem actually means "house of bread."
- Make a recording of a newborn to play low in the background. You can get these online, but find one that is just the gentle sounds that a baby makes and not the hungry screams of discontent.

Before you leave the room, lead the kids in kneeling at the manger. Pray together, enthusiastically rejoicing at how much God loves each of us (but don't wake the baby). The only thing to "ask" in this time of prayer is that God would make Himself real to each child and that the children would chase after Jesus as their Savior and Lord all their lives. This is the start of Jesus' life, and it can be the start of a child's new life in Him. End the time of prayer with a commitment to keep Jesus foremost in your Christmas celebration!

THE 12 SOCKS OF CHRISTMAS

Supplies:

- 6 pair of children's socks
- Command hooks

I once heard Dr. James Dobson say that one of the most important things you can give your kids is **tradition**. Those words made my ears perk up because I'm a person who enjoys change. He went on to say that tradition gives kids a sense of belonging to something that has happened for years and will continue to happen. Tradition is something they can count on, and in this world of rapid change, it's nice to know there are some things you can be sure will be the same.

This activity can be done with a small group, as a family, or as something unique that grandparents can do to make special memories with their grandchildren during the Christmas season.

Purchase 6 pairs of new children's socks—a variety of patterns are fun. Actually get the size the kids who are participating would wear, because when all the activities are done, they will be able to use them.

Hang the 12 individual socks in a prominent place. (I use the Command hooks to put them in the front hallway, and then I can easily take them down when the decorations come down.)

Instead of observing the 12 Days of Christmas in between Thanksgiving and Christmas Eve, we do the 12 Socks of Christmas. Each sock contains a card with special instructions for an activity you can do together. The activities that can be written on the cards are endless! Some take a time commitment. Others only take a few minutes. Some can be costly, while others are free. It's up to you what you put on the sock cards! Here are some ideas to get you started:

- With our grandchildren, the first sock opened always indicates a gift to open under the tree (which is a pair of Christmas pajamas) and spending the night.
- A trip to Bass Pro Shop. If you have one of these stores in your area, their tradition is to give their community a wonderful children's Christmas area. Of course, the kids can try out new toys the store has for sale, but it's really a fun couple of hours.
- Go shopping to fill an Operation Christmas Child shoebox.
- Have a Christmas tea. Everyone wears Santa hats (or other dress-up hats). You don't have to have fancy foods; just chop everything they like into small chunks and put them on a 3-tier serving tower. Serve hot chocolate in small teacups.
- Make a Christmas ornament.
- Open a gift that is a Christmas book and snuggle up to read it together.
- Go to the theater for a Christmas play or movie.
- Make gifts, or go shopping, for their mom and dad.
- Count all the nativities in the house and that you see throughout the entire day.
- Hang candy canes all over the church or house and have the kids go on a candy cane hunt.

- Watch marshmallows get huge in the microwave…and then eat the yummy, sticky treats.
- Pray in candlelight.
- Play with making videotapes of the kids sharing Christmas greetings and singing Christmas carols.
- Make green Rice Krispie treats and use a cookie cutter to make them into Christmas trees. Then decorate them with little candies.
- Drive around town and look for Christmas lights.
- Make a peppermint tree. You need a Styrofoam cone, straight pins, and wrapped peppermints. Use straight pins to make a ring of peppermint candies around the base of the Styrofoam cone. Make the next ring in the same way so that the peppermints barely overlap the ring below it. Continue doing this until the cone is completely covered. Add a few red bows and you have an edible decoration that will come in handy after those big Christmas meals.
- Set up all the nativities you have. Take time to play with them as you do and encourage the kids to retell the story.
- Instead of making a gingerbread house, use the same kind of ingredients to create the manger scene.
- Bake cookies together and then visit an assisted living facility to personally deliver them to the residents face-to-face.

Christmas Storybook

One of my all-time favorite books to recommend at Christmas is *The Last Straw* by Fredrick Thury.

NEW YEAR'S DAY

Psalm 31:15 – Plenty of Time
Jeremiah 29:11 – Traffic Cone Plans
Lamentations 3:22-23 – Do Overs
2 Corinthians 5:17 – Butterfly Garden

VALENTINE'S DAY

Deuteronomy 6:5 – Bobbing Love
Deuteronomy 10:12 – Heart Wallpaper
Isaiah 43:1 – Musical Hearts
Romans 5:8 – Krispie Valentine Treats

ST. PATRICK'S DAY

Genesis 50:20 – You Meant It for Harm
Matthew 3:16-17 – Apple Shamrocks
Acts 1:8 – Shamrock Cupcakes
Romans 10:15 – Good News Feet

APRIL FOOL'S DAY

Matthew 7:24-27 – What a Mess!
Matthew 28:6 – Gotcha
Luke 6:31 – Spewing Foolishness
Luke 12:16-21 – Potato Pull
1 Corinthians 15:55 – Gotcha

EASTER

Matthew 5:14 & 16 – After Dark Egg Hunt
Luke 22:7-38 – It All Happened at Dinner
John 8:12 – After Dark Egg Hunt
John 13:1-30 – It All Happened at Dinner
John 19:2-3 – Thorns and Jewels
John 19:16-18 – Hammering the Spike
1 Peter 5:4 – Thorns and Jewels

EARTH DAY

Genesis 1:26 – Food Creation Menagerie
Deuteronomy 11:12 – Picnic Project
Psalm 1:1-3 – Crystal Tree
John 1:3 – Earthy Scavenger Hunt
Ephesians 2:10 – Picnic Project

MOTHER'S DAY

Proverbs 17:22a – Make Mom Laugh
Proverbs 31:25 – Make Mom Laugh
Proverbs 31:28 – Hats Off to Moms
Luke 2:19 – Stained Glass Heart
2 Timothy 1:5 – Flower Legacy

MEMORIAL DAY

Joshua 4:9 – Stones of Remembrance
Luke 22:19-20 – Red Poppy
Hebrews 8:12 – Flush it!
Hebrews 12:1 – Cloud of Witnesses Poster

FATHER'S DAY

Exodus 20:12 – Honor with Art
Deuteronomy 1:29-31 – Carry Me
Proverbs 3:11-12 – Sanding Discipline
Isaiah 40:11 – Carry Me
Malachi 4:6a – Game Show Golf
Hebrews 12:10b – Sanding Discipline

JULY 4TH

John 8:31-32 – Untangled Freedom
John 8:32 – Fireworks
Galatians 5:13 – Freedom to Serve
2 Corinthians 3:17 - Secret Worship

LABOR DAY

Proverbs 16:3 – Kick It Over to God
Romans 4:4 – Work Hard, Be Generous
1 Corinthians 10:31 – Growing Ice
Ephesians 4:28 – Work Hard, Be Generous
Colossians 3:23 – Hammering Heart

HALLOWEEN

Ezekiel 37:11, Ezekiel 37:14 – Dry Bones
John 3:16-17 – Pumpkin Gospel
2 Corinthians 5:17 – Pumpkin Gospel
2 Timothy 1:7 – Crush Fear
James 1:2-4 – Obstacles Galore

VETERANS DAY

2 Samuel 22:2-4 – Build a Fortress
John 12:26 – Follow and Serve
John 15:13 – Belly Crawl
Ephesians 6:11 & 15 – Shoes of Peace

THANKSGIVING

Psalm 28:7 – Covered with Thanksgiving
Psalm 40:5 – Cornucopias
John 14:15 – To Bend or Not to Bend
1 Thessalonians 5:18 – Marshmallow Madness

CHRISTMAS

Matthew 2:9 – Hovering Bottle
Luke 2:1-20 – All other activities

WORKS CITED

DeCosta-Klipa, Nik. "Why Fireworks on the Fourth of July? John Adams, That's Why" *Boston.com*. Boston Globe Media Partners, LLC, 2 July 2015. Web. 10 Nov. 2015.

"Earth Day: The History of a Movement." *Earth Day Network Main*. Web. 10 Nov. 2015.

Heneghan, Tom. "Reported Christian 'martyr' Deaths Double in 2013: Report." *Reuters*. Thomson Reuters, 8 Jan. 2014. Web. 11 Nov. 2015.

"History of Valentine's Day." *History.com*. A+E Networks, 2009. Web. 10 Nov. 2015.

"Infoplease Article." Fact Monster. © 2000–2013 Sandbox Networks,Inc., publishing as Fact Monster. 11 Nov. 2015 <http://www.factmonster.com/spot/hotdog1.html>.

"Labor Day." *History.com*. A&E Television Networks, 2010. Web. 10 Nov. 2015.

"The Origins of Veterans Day." *Celebrating America's Freedoms*. U.S. Department of Veterans Affairs. Web. 10 Nov. 2015. <http:/www.va.gov/opa/publications/celebrate/vetday.pdf>.

ten Boom, Corrie. *The Hiding Place*. Bantam Books; Reprint edition (October 1, 1974)

NOTES

NOTES

www.ingramcontent.com/pod-product-compliance
Lightning Source LLC
Chambersburg PA
CBHW080944280925
33254CB00005B/26

* 9 7 8 1 6 8 4 3 4 2 4 5 7 *